The Catholic Priest: His Identity and Values

A Ministerial Profile of the Joliet Presbyterate

John C. Fogarty, O. Carm., D. Min.

Sheed & Ward

Sheed & Ward™ is a service of National Catholic Reporter
Publishing Company, Inc.

Library of Congress Catalog Card Number: 88- 63968

ISBN: 1-55612-218-7

Published by: Sheed & Ward
                115 E. Armour Blvd. P.O. Box 419492
                Kansas City, MO 64141-6492

To order, call: (800) 333-7373

To ALL those
who have enabled me
to be the person
I have become.

To Judy Vera
Who would have thought
it would come to this? I
shall always be grateful for
your help.

Sincerely,
Fr. John C. Fogarty, O. Carm.

Contents

Acknowledgements

This major project has been a long time aborning—three and one half years in fact. Certainly that must be a record of some sort and worthy of the Guinness Book of Records. For a variety of reasons my attempts to finish the project within the first year after completing the course work were frustrated. And the story has been the same since then, until recently. This past June I was given permission to go on Sabbatical. After a well deserved, extended vacation, I settled down to complete the project. Within a few weeks, I was asked to substitute for one of our pastors who had suffered a stroke. Fortunately the stroke was not so severe as it could have been. Fr. Franklin Tasker, O. Carm., Pastor of St. Matthew Church in Glendale Heights, Illinois, was able to return to active duty at Thanksgiving. I continued there in residence while completing the work on this major project. For his encouragement and support, as well as that of the other members of the Carmelite community there, I am most grateful.

I owe a debt of gratitude to the many people who were, in one way or another, involved in my effort to obtain the Doctor of Ministry degree. Among these are: Most Rev. Joseph L. Imesch, Bishop of Joliet, who gave permission for the program to be inaugurated at St. Charles Borromeo Pastoral Center in Romeoville in 1981 and who provided some financial assistance from diocesan funds to the priests enrolled in the program; to my Carmelite Superiors, past and present, especially the Most Rev. John Malley, O.Carm., the Very Rev. Paul T. Hoban, O.Carm., and the Very Rev. Murray W. Phelan, O.Carm., as well as my Carmelite confrères, all of whom, by reason of their support and encouragement, assisted me greatly; to my co-learners whose names are found at the end of their statement and who cooperated to the fullest extent possible in their role as co-learners.

I would be remiss if I were to neglect the Carmelite community in Washington, D.C. They were the quintessence of hospitality during my two-month stay there while doing some research for the first chapter of this project. Dr. Donald W. Buggert, O.Carm., assistant professor of Systematic Theology at the Washington Theological Union, provided me with invaluable assistance in the development of that part of the project.

I wish to express my thanks to my advisor, Dr. Patricia Smith, R.S.M., for the support, direction and encouragement she has given me these past three years; to the Institute for Continuing Education Administration, especially Dr. Mary Chupein, S.F.C.C., our "mentress" during the two years of course work; to Rev. Dr. Anthony Vader of the Chicago Archdiocese for allowing me to model my questionnaire after the one he had constructed as part of his doctoral dissertation at Loyola University, Chicago; to Sister Marie Augusta Neal, Professor of Sociology at Emmanuel College, Boston, Massachusetts, for her kind assistance in the early stages of this project; to Dr. Michael Reich for critiquing my questionnaire; to Dr. Paul Kaiser for his help with the questionnaire and for supervising the compute-related work it required.

A special word of appreciation is due to all the members of the Joliet Presbyterate who cooperated with me so willingly and promptly in this project. Finally, I am grateful to Dr. Rosann Catalano, my reader, to Nancy Moody, who collated much of the material in Sections V, VI, and VII, and to Judy Vera, who very graciously agreed to type the final version of this project.

Introduction

Background and Statement of the Problem

More than a decade ago, the National Opinion Research Center submitted the results of its study of Catholic priests in the United States to the United States Conference of Catholic Bishops. The third and final segment of a series,[1] it was published in 1972 under the title *The Catholic Priest in the United States: Sociological Investigations*. The work was hailed as a significant contribution to a better understanding of the priest and his role in the Catholic Church of the United States. And so it was. Comprehensive and exhaustive, it painted a realistic picture of the background, thinking and attitudes of almost six thousand priests, including a number who had resigned from priestly ministry.

[1]National Opinion Research Center, *The Catholic Priest in the United States: Sociological Investigations* (Washington: USCC, 1972). The third segment was produced by the Center. The second segment, also published in 1972, was the work of two authors—Eugene C. Kennedy and Victor J. Heckler, *The Catholic Priest in the United States: Psychological Investigations* (Washington: USCC, 1972). The first segment had appeared in the previous year. John Tracy Ellis, ed., *The Catholic*

Some of the turmoil the Church experienced in the 1970's has now subsided. The impression that things are changing too rapidly is no longer with us. At the same time, most would probably agree that we have not reached another plateau, that we are still in a period of transition. All is not well, all is not perfectly calm. Some of the older questions remain, and there are new ones, too, such as—why *do* priests stay?

The motivations which priests have for remaining active in priestly ministry is an aspect with which the National Opinion Research Center did not deal. There has been little, if any, investigation of this subject. I believe that it would be worthwhile to pursue the matter further, though not in so thorough and detailed a way as the National Opinion Research Center did its work. The present study provides some understanding of the ideas and feelings of a fairly good sampling of priests working in the 1980's, and includes their reasons for remaining active in priestly ministry as well as certain other aspects of their lives, such as their theology of priesthood, ministerial and personal practices, sources of stress and their attitude toward vocation recruitment.

With this in mind, I intend to delineate some of the traditional and contemporary roles of priests in this century, give the results of a questionnaire administered to the priests working in the Diocese of Joliet, Illinois, in 1984, and then offer a commentary and an analysis of the results obtained from the questionnaires that were returned. Such a study will, I believe, be of service to the Joliet Diocesan Personnel Board and to the Presbyteral Council, as well as to the larger Local Church of Joliet. There is also the possibility that it could be of some value to the Bishop's Committee on Priestly Formation (cf. Appendix A).

1.

Theological, Pastoral and Ministerial Issues

The Way We Were (1900-1950)

The purpose of this portion of my study is to provide the reader with an essentially phenomenological, not an evaluative, description of the role of the priest in the first half of the present century, as that role was perceived by the Catholic population and by priests themselves. I shall conclude with a sketch of the theological setting of the period, together with an analysis of some of the theological themes then in vogue. To achieve this, I will offer some reflections based on my own experience during the last two decades of the period under discussion and on material that I have read in connection with this project.

1

Any movement, any era cannot be looked at in isolation. A particular date or event may be singled out to mark its beginning or end, but that is a purely arbitrary decision. The roots of the movement or era are to be found in the period of history that preceded it, and its effects will still be present in some form long after it has receded into the background. Such is the case with the role of the priest during the first half of the twentieth century. It was shaped and influenced by the events that occurred and the attitudes that were prevalent during the decades of the nineteenth century.

In *Theology of Ministry*, Thomas F. O'Meara devotes a chapter to the six metamorphoses of ministry that have occurred within the Church over the course of its history. The sixth, referred to as the "romanticization of ministry," began in the nineteenth century and lasted into the middle of the twentieth. Thus, it includes the period that comes within the scope of this portion of the study. O'Meara comments at one point:

...But when hopes of restoration if not renewal and transformation cooled after 1848, other faces of the Roman Catholic Church in the nineteenth century showed themselves. There was, first of all, a distrust of the world, society and state. Since the looked-for renewal and expansion of Catholic life did not occur in the structure of a church again excessively Roman, mysticism rather than ministry was cultivated. The literature of piety in France during the seventeenth and eighteenth centuries prepared for a limitation and individualization of the priesthood. The priest was placed in a mystical niche, exalted, described as metaphysically equal to, even higher than, angelic beings. He lost his roots in the community and in the wider, diverse church. His power in the Eucharist and in penance seemed personal gifts without any source in word or community. Bishops and priests moved or were moved to the edge of society. There they experienced their powerlessness. They nourished a theology of the world as sinful, and they turned inward in their theology of the Kingdom of God to a spirituality of the soul in prayer.[1]

Among the luminaries of the nineteenth century that O'Meara mentions further on in his work is Lacordaire, the famous Dominican preacher at the Cathedral of Notre Dame in Paris. Lacordaire's name was not unfamiliar to priests during the first half of the present century. His paean on priesthood was often utilized by newly ordained priests on the cards commemorating their ordination. Quite frequently the priest who was invited to preach on the occasion of a "First Mass" would make use of Lacordaire's words in order to end his sermon on a highly emotional note. The following quotation synthesizes quite well the idealistic view of priesthood that was current, not only during Lacordaire's time, but well into the present century:

> To live in the midst of the world without wishing its pleasures; to be a member of each family, yet belonging to none; to share all sufferings; to penetrate all secrets; to heal ll wounds; to go from men to God and offer Him their prayers; to return from God to men to bring pardon and hope; to have a heart of fire for charity and a heart of bronze for chastity; to teach and to pardon, to console and bless always. My God, what a life! And it is yours, O Priest of Jesus Christ![2]

Nor need we hearken back to former times in order to find such expressions of this idealism with regard to priesthood. In 1950 the same basic concepts were being presented by well-known Catholic writers and lecturers such as Catherine de Hueck Doherty. Quoting a Dr. Powers, Kennedy and Heckler give an outline of Mrs. Doherty's thoughts on the subject as follows:

> For a priest is a miracle of God's love to us; a man who, through his sacrament of ordination, becomes *another Christ* with powers that beggar human imagination...Nothing can be greater in this world of ours than a priest. Nothing But God Himself. A priest is a holy man because he walks before the Face of the All Holy. A priest understands all things. A priest forgives all things. A priest is a man who lives to serve. A priest is a man who has crucified himself, so that he too may be lifted up and draw all things to Christ. A priest is a symbol of the Word made Flesh. A priest is the naked sword of God's Justice. A priest is the hand of God's mercy. A priest is the reflection of God's love. He teaches God to us...he brings God to us...he represents God to us.[3]

The expression of such ideas as these, putting heavy emphasis on the "ideal priest," exerted a great deal of pressure on priests, not simply to *strive* toward the ideal, but to *realize* it in their own lives. A situation was created in which the priest was seen to be "different" from all other mortals. Thus, the atmosphere in which a priest lived and worked was an atmosphere of what I would term "differentiation." He was made to appear "different" because of the high expectations placed on him, not only by those in authority, but also by the faithful who perceived him as "another Christ."

What were the sources of this separation, this differentiation on the part of the Catholic population? A partial answer, I submit, is to be found in the fact that the priest occupied a special status within the community, was invested with awesome powers, and exercised tremendous spiritual authority over the community.

One sometimes hears or reads that, for at least the first few decades of this century, the Church was basically an "immigrant" church. Most of the people who came to America from other countries in the latter part of the last century and the first part of this century were at a loss as to how to find their way in this "land of opportunity." Many did not speak the language; most, if not all, experienced the prejudice manifested by those whose ancestors had come to this country at an earlier date. Bewildered by many problems, they searched for an anchor, a beacon of hope that would enable them to survive and, in due time, to prosper. They found their anchor, their beacon, in the closest tie with their past, the Church, and especially in its local representative, the priest. Because of his education and training, because of his position within the community, people looked to him for comfort, for assistance, for direction.

James Mohler described well the role of the priest during this period when he wrote:

> ...Even fifty years ago the local pastor with his seminary training was one of the best educated men in town. When most of the laity had at best a high school education, mothers saw in their children's vocation to the ministry a step up the social ladder into the professional class. The clergy were consulted on all sides from moral questions to problems in economics or politics.[4]

Ordinary members of the believing community found a great deal of solace in the practice of their religion. For them it served as a nexus to their native land. The perception of the priest that they had inherited from those who had gone before them did not change at all by reason of their coming to America. At an early age they had been taught that a priest was deserving of great respect. He was the one who was able to bring Jesus Himself down to them on the altar during the Holy Sacrifice of the Mass; he was the one who received Holy Communion, not annually, not monthly, not weekly, but daily; he was the one who could absolve them from their sins and restore them to God's Grace. His hands, and his alone, were consecrated and able to touch the Body of Christ and thus those hands were to be kissed by "unworthy sinners" such as they, not only on the day of a priest's ordination, but at other times as well.

The influence of the First Vatican Council's declaration concerning the Pope's infallibility was very much in the foreground of Catholic thought and practice during this period. At a time when people were seeking their identity through institutions, most Catholics found their ready acceptance of this dogma to be a way of seeing themselves as special. No other church made such a claim as theirs did. They were quite willing to accept the idea that the Pope, by reason of his role as the "Vicar of Christ on earth and the successor of St. Peter," could not err when he spoke "ex cathedra" on matters of faith and morals.

Nor did the people confine their understanding of the dogma of infallibility to the limits imposed on it by the Council Fathers. Many gave the same weight to other papal pronouncements, especially papal encyclicals. That particular attitude has perdured in some areas even to this day (e.g., the popular understanding of "Humanae Vitae").

Because of the close identification between the pope and the bishops, as well as between the bishops and their priests, the force of this authority filtered down to the local level. Most people considered the priest's word to be law. If he said that something was a sin, it was. When he preached from the pulpit, an aura of infallibility surrounded his every word. There was no need to question, no need to doubt.

As the twentieth century advanced, Catholics in the United States began to find their place in the sun of American society. Better jobs came along, more education became readily available. They lost their immigrant status and began to be absorbed into the mainstream of American life. In the thirties and forties, upward mobility became a reality. Now the male children in a Catholic family could aspire to become doctors, lawyers and priests. All three professions were seen to be worth striving for because of the power and prestige associated with them. Those who became priests were placed on a pedestal and were truly "set apart." This was the way in which most people perceived their priests and, in general, this was the way in which priests perceived themselves.

By reason of their ordination to the priesthood, priests saw themselves as being radically different from the laity. For the most part, they were able to identify their personality with their role and so considered themselves separated from the faithful because they were certain of their special identity, they were committed to leading a celibate life, and they were intimately associated with an institution that promoted a specific set of values and gloried in the fact that immutability was one of its chief attributes.

The priest of this era was frequently told and firmly believed that he was "another Christ." He acted in the name and with the authority of Jesus Himself. All things being equal, he was able to trace his priestly lineage back through time to the Apostles, not by reason of his birth, as was the case with the Levitical priesthood, but by reason of his sacramental ordination that had been established by Jesus at the Last Supper. Hearing or reading such an idea as "a significant fact of Calvary might easily escape us: that from the cross

Christ confided his mother to a priest—a newly ordained priest, the sacerdotal seal still fresh upon his soul,"[5] caused the priest no problem whatsoever. The same could be said of the following passage:

> From the fact of Christ's election of just twelve Apostles, whatever may have been His reason or purpose in the choice of that particular number, certainly we can think of those twelve Apostles as the twelve girders or I-beams which form the basic framework of the Church and give strength and shape to that grand edifice.
>
> Every priest is a successor of the Apostles. Every priest is a lineal extension of one of those twelve beams which formed the original structure of Christ's Church. Our priesthood is the framework about which the Church is built and without which the Church could not stand or perdure.[6]

In his role as confector of sacraments the priest found his most intimate union with his Lord. He could resonate well with the words of Archbishop Schulte of Indianapolis, who, in his introduction to *Essays on the Priesthood* wrote: "Our mission is to bring sanctity into the souls of men. This is effected for the most part by the sacraments if the subject is rightly disposed."[7]

Especially in terms of his celebration of Mass was the priest conscious of the intimate relationship he enjoyed with Christ. He alone could touch and fix his gaze upon the Sacred Species. With his back to the people, his body taking the place of the screen utilized in the Eastern Rite liturgy, he would allow people only a fleeting glance at the Host and the Chalice during the Elevation. Later, at the "Ecce, Agnus Dei," he would turn to the people with the Body of Christ held between his fingers, but they were supposed to bow their heads and beat their breasts as a sign of their unworthiness.

In much the same way the priest sensed this intimate bond in his administration of the Sacrament of Penance. By reason of the power to forgive sins that had been conferred on him at ordination, he alone could bind and loose; he alone could serve as judge and jury. His main task was to make certain that the penitent confessed his sins according to genus, species and number. Provided that the penitent was truly sorry for his sins and had a firm purpose of amendment, the priest could then pronounce the words of absolution in the name of Jesus: "*Ego* te absolvo ab omnibus peccatis tuis in nomine Patris, et Fillii, et Spiritus Sancti. Amen."

During this period a priest knew exactly what was expected of him. His job description was quite clear and definite. He celebrated Mass each day, recited the entire Divine Office for that day under pain of mortal sin, taught religion to the school children a few times each week, served as moderator for the Holy Name Society or the Ladies' Sodality, conducted a novena service and/or a holy hour each week, was on duty for office calls or emergencies, visited the hospitals, and heard confessions regularly on Saturday afternoons for two hours and again for two hours in the evening, as well as on the eve of First Fridays.

When a parishioner came to make arrangements for a wedding, the procedure the priest followed was quite simple. He would ascertain that both parties were old enough and free to marry. Then he would have them fill out the necessary forms and set the time for the wedding rehearsal and for the wedding as well. If one of the parties was not a Catholic, he was required to give that person a series of instructions dealing with the beliefs of Catholics. He made certain that this individual promised in writing under oath that any children born of the union would be baptized and raised as Catholics. Until the late forties, he was also required to inform the couple that they would have to be married in the rectory, since the church could be used only when both parties were of the Catholic faith. Such was the extent of the priest's involvement in marriage preparation.

Even for the wedding itself he was not required to inject his own personality. He simply read verbatim the "Exhortation Before Marriage." Here, as in the Eucharist and Penance, his involvement had a robot-like, mechanistic quality to it. That, one would imagine, should be expected since the sacraments were confected "ex opere operato."

Except for his day off and his annual vacation, the priest's life was, for the most part, centered in the rectory, the parish school and the church. The structured routine of his seminary days, which had been modeled on life in a monastery, was still very much a part of his life. A "secular" priest he was not.

A priest's association with people in the parish was quite limited. When he would visit their homes, there was usually an official dimension to his presence in their midst. Someone in the family was ill or dying and so in need of the Sacraments; a census of the entire parish was being taken up; the annual canvassing of the parish for special donations was under way. Always conscious of his priestly role in these situations, he could relax and be himself only when he was with his own family or with his fellow priests.

His commitment to celibacy also contributed to his self-understanding as someone "set apart." The majority of the human race married and had families. He, however, had been called to a "higher state of life." Well aware, at least intellectually, of the sacrificial dimension involved, he embraced a celibate life style in order to demonstrate his regard for a Church law that would enable him to be free to be "all things to all men."

His extremely close association with an institution that promoted a specific set of values also contributed to the priest's special identity. Those values were readily accessible to him in the Code of Canon Law and in the theology manuals. The principles enunciated therein had universal application. When any question concerning faith or morals arose, only one thing was necessary—consult the Code or the manuals. There one could find a definitive answer that was applicable to each and every case.

Immutability, as well as indefectibility, was an attribute of the Church that helped many set it apart from other institutions. The seasons changed, time marched on, but the Church remained essentially the same in all places and for all times. Such a quality provided comfort and identity to all associated with it, especially priests. The language the Church employed, the beliefs it held, the customs it observed had been unchanged for so many centuries that one had the impression it was ever thus. Creativity was neither desired, nor encouraged, nor practiced. The Church was indeed a rock. Like Gibraltar, it was solid, impregnable, unchangeable.

This static state of affairs as far as religious beliefs were concerned was due, at least in part, to the approach that was taken with regard to the study of religion in general and theology in particular. In Catholic high schools and colleges, apologetics was considered to be the most practical method of preserving the faith of students. The authors of the textbooks and the teachers were intent upon putting forward the most cogent proofs based on reason for such topics as the existence of God, the Divinity of Christ, the miracles of Jesus, etc. The main objective of these books and the courses offered was to further strengthen the faith of these youthful believers. If they questioned or failed to accept the proffered proofs, they were considered to be "lost souls."

Those who entered the seminary received much the same training on both the high school and college level. When the time came for them to study theology, a similar approach was taken. Sacred Scripture, the Fathers of the Church, the declarations of the Councils, and the teachings of the Popes were cited as "proofs" for every and all doctrinal issues. An appeal to reason was the ancillary method employed in the treatment of all dogmatic questions. The material was arranged in a series of theses. All one had to do was to memorize the information the manuals provided and all would be well.

This approach reflected an attitude that had been prevalent even in the previous century. In *Man Becoming,* Gregory Baum summarizes well the mood that was current then and that lasted well into the first half of the twentieth century. He comments:

> uring the nineteenth century, wrestling with the issues raised by rationalism and fideism and resisting the extremes of both, Catholic theologians had introduced a radical distinction between faith and its rational credibility. They acknowledged with the entire Christian tradition that faith is a free gift of God and hence essentially indemonstrable. Yet what can be demonstrated, they added, is the divine origin of the message believed by faith. What can be proven, ultimately by reference to miracles, is that the message preached by the Church is not of human making; it is a divine message and hence, however startling to the human intelligence, it is worthy of belief or is credible... The price that Catholic theologians had to pay for the solution of separating faith and credibility was the exclusion of God's revelation from the spiritual process by which man comes to know what is important and true. According to the official theology of the nineteenth century, there was no inner continuity between

the rational discernment of credibility and the Spirit-created acknowledgement of the divine Word. In other words, the credibility of faith remained totally extrinsic to faith itself.[8]

This notion of extrinsicism permeated much of the theology of both eras. Especially in regard to God Himself, the pedagogical approach employed placed a heavy emphasis on God's transcendence. He was understood to be someone who was above, beyond, outside, over against and unrelated to us, our history and the world in which we live. He was the Supreme Being who "dwelt in unapproachable light." One could catch glimpses of His power and majesty in the awesome beauty of His created effects—the sun, the moon, the stars, the sky, the earth, and even in human beings. People reached out to Him primarily in those brief moments of contact experienced through prayer and the reception of the sacraments. Though God made us "to know Him, to love Him, and to serve Him in this world," we really were not able to know Him as we know ourselves. That knowledge was reserved for the "next world" where we, seeing Him face to face, would finally experience true happiness. In this life, God would always be the "distant Mystery."

With such an extrinsic view of God, one should not be surprised to find that theologians, as well as theological students, adopted a similar attitude toward Jesus Christ. Though Sunday after Sunday they professed their faith in Him as "true God and true man," they paid scant attention to His humanity and concentrated, instead, on His divinity. Naturally, His eternal and personal pre-existence was presumed. They faithfully followed the Council of Chalcedon, which had made use of the terms "person" and "nature," as understood in Hellenistic philosophy, to confess and "explain" the mystery of the God-Man, Jesus Christ.

For classical theologians since Origen, the most important moment in the history of the human race was the Incarnation. Though Jesus' life, death and resurrection were highlighted in the Church's liturgy and were considered to be central elements of the Catholic faith, nonetheless, these events had no significant relationship to Jesus' divine Sonship, i.e., his unique relationship to God. The attention paid to the Incarnation as proof of God's love for us was caused, not so much by St. Francis' popularization of the creche, as by theologians' and preachers' stress on the divinity of Jesus which was fully established in the first moment of his human origins by virtue of his pre-existence with the Father.

Most of the faithful looked upon Jesus as totally different from all other humans. Even reclining in the crib, Jesus knew everything. From the very first moment of his life here on earth, he enjoyed the Beatific Vision. He *appeared* to be perfectly human, but he was really God in a human body. Objectively speaking, there was present in their thinking an heretical tinge of Docetism, since they perceived this Jesus as lacking a genuinely human psychology. This Jesus could not *really* be ignorant, could not *really* be tempted, could not *really* suffer and die. Such was the lot of the rest of humanity. The Son of God was the exception.

Why then had Jesus come into our midst? His primary purpose was to bring us to salvation and to reveal to us certain divine truths, truths that we were incapable of discovering on our own. There is much biblical "evidence" to support every claim he made about himself and his mission, e.g., the Virgin Birth, the adoration of the Magi, the knowledge and wisdom he possessed at an early age, his prophecies and his miracles and, especially, his resurrection. All of these factors contributed to the idea that Jesus, though supposedly human, was not really like the rest of us.

Such a Christology "from above," that began with and emphasized the divinity of Christ and the incarnation, obviously colored the classical perception of Jesus Christ. Small wonder it was that many understood him to be so separated from the rest of humanity.

The same approach was taken by classical theologians with regard to such subjects as Grace, the Bible, and the Church. Because of the metaphysical mind-set out of which they operated, they saw Grace as a "thing" which came to people from without. The Bible was basically a record of God's word spoken from Heaven to the human race on earth. The Church, over which popes, bishops and their duly constituted representatives presided, was seen as a divinely instituted structure that had as its primary purpose, the task of keeping people not only uncontaminated in a world full of evil, but also well prepared for their entrance into the Kingdom of God in the life to come.

With regard to the theology of priesthood, we have already seen that it had an "other-worldly" quality to it that reflects the classical approach to theology. Whatever was written about priesthood had no distinctively American quality to it. Most of the publications on this subject were simply French or German translations, many of which had been written in the previous century. These, as well as the few that were published originally in English by such writers as Boyland and Nash, dealt principally with the priest's own spirituality. They were intent upon assisting him in his ascent up the ladder of personal perfection. Concern for the world and the Church's mission to society did not seem to warrant much attention.

The same thing could be said with regard to the social encyclicals of Leo XIII and Pius XI. They received scant notice. Though they had been proclaimed from the mountain tops, the people in the valleys below were too far removed to hear the message that was being communicated from above. Only gradually, toward the latter part of this period, with the advent of such movements as the Young Christian Workers, the Young Christian Students and Catholic Action— all greatly influenced by Canon Cardijn's Jocist Movement that had begun in Belgium and blossomed inother parts of Europe—did the word begin to spread from below that there truly was a social dimension to the Gospel message.

For the most part, the men who served the Church during this period, some of whom are still alive and active in the ministry, were good men, dedicated to their work and bent on serving the Lord to the best of their abilities. They were the products of their own period of history. They could not have had the same vision or the same knowledge that is available today, because neither had yet surfaced to any great degree. The winds of change were, however, already stirring, especially during the last two decades of this period. With the fifties and sixties came the latest evolution.

The Way We Are Becoming (1950-1984)

First of all, I should like to point out that my use of the progressive form in the title of this section was most deliberate. I wish to make it perfectly clear that we are in a period of transition and probably will be for some time to come. Thus, it is impossible to give an objective, complete analysis of priesthood as it exists today, because we are standing in the midst of the trees that comprise the forest.

Before moving on to a discussion of priestly ministry from 1950 to the present, let me summarize the first section of this paper. We have examined the role of the priest in the United States from 1900 to 1950. The priests of that era exercised their ministry in an atmosphere of "differentiation," because people perceived them to be a "cut above" everyone else. Priests had a special status within the community, were looked up to as "other Christ," and exercised spiritual authority over the lives of their flocks. The priests also made their contribution to this atmosphere because they saw themselves as people "set apart." They identified themselves with their role, which was to confect the Sacraments, fulfill specific tasks, proclaim a definite set of values and preserve the "status quo." Finally, we attempted to show that this situation was rooted in the popular understanding of certain theological concepts concerning God, Jesus Christ, Grace, the Bible and the Church.

In this section, again relying heavily on my own experience in recent years, especially in light of the Doctor of Ministry Program, I would like to examine some of the elements that contributed to the changes that have occurred in society, look at some shifts in understanding of certain theological concepts that have taken place, describe people's present perception of the clergy, as well as priests' perception of themselves, and, finally, locate Pope John Paul's vision of priesthood in this period of the Church's history.

To expand on some of the basic changes that have occurred in our society would be to belabor the obvious. The general "knowledge explosion" in all fields of human endeavor has had a marked effect on our view of ourselves and the world in which we live. It has also had an influence on the way in which we perceive God, Jesus Christ, the Church and her fairly visible local representatives—the priests.

Among the many factors that contributed to this different understanding of spiritual realities were a sense of openness, the development of an appreciation for history and historical consciousness, the decline of common meaning and the practical implementation of certain principles that had been enunciated by the Second Vatican Council. Let us consider each of these elements.

The fact that people were faced with so many changes in society about which they could do nothing contributed to their sense of openness to change. Moreover, many Christians discovered that this new sense of openness was affecting their view of truth itself. In *Man Becoming,* Gregory Baum refers to this new sense of universal brotherhood that Christians were experiencing. He writes:

> ...Secondly, in recent decades Christians have discovered a new openness to truth. Christ summons them to be open to the truth, even the painful truth, wherever it addresses them. Christians realize that they have learned much in the past, that they have often changed their minds, and hence they expect that this will continue in the future. As they enter into conversation with others or reflect on personal experience and political conditions, they remain open to the new that is being uttered to them. They no longer feel that they possess a complete system of truths, in the light of which they are to evaluate their experiences of reality; they are open to the new which they hear, even when it hurts, even when it shatters some of their inherited ideas, so long as it ties in with their deepest convictions about Jesus Christ. Catholics have become listeners, critical listeners. They test what they hear, they try it on, they see whether it fits in with their conscience and fosters the growth and reconciliation to which Christ summons them. If it does, they acknowledge the truth ad-

dressed to them and allow it to qualify their understanding of reality.[9]

For Catholics, the development of a sense of history, especially as it manifested itself in the field of theology, had far reaching effects on their view of reality as well. In the past, historical events had been examined in much the same way as a scientist would view a specimen under a microscope. These events had been inspected in isolation. No attention was paid to the language spoken at that time, to the meaning words conveyed, to the values that were prevalent, or to the culture out of which people operated.

Now, however, the situation was changing dramatically. To demonstrate that what was going on was evolutionary, rather than revolutionary, one has only to recall that a change had already begun in the 1940's with regard to the approach Catholic biblical scholars were allowed to take in studying Sacred Scripture. In 1943, Pope Pius XII issued his encyclical *Divino Afflante Spiritu* in which he granted these scholars permission to employ the historical-critical method in their work. At long last, Catholic biblical scholars could join their Protestant counterparts who had already made great strides in their understanding of Scripture because of their freedom to make use of the historical-critical method.

In other branches of theology the same approach was being taken. Theologians had become somewhat reluctant to simply reiterate the statements of Ephesus, Chalcedon and the other Councils, as if the final word had been pronounced about a particular dogma formulated centuries before. Their comprehensive study of those eras that had produced these dogmas showed that the Council Fathers and theologians of that time had been heavily influenced by the language, meaning, values and culture of their particular period of history. The theologians of our own day had to wait until 1973 to receive official approval from Rome for their efforts. In that year, the Sacred Congregation for the Doctrine of the Faith issued a document entitled *Mysterium Ecclesiae,* which, among other issues, dealt with the cultural circumscription of dogma. It stated that:

> the transmission of Divine Revelation by the Church encounters difficulties of various kinds. These arise from the fact that the hidden mysteries of God "by their very nature so far transcend the human intellect that even if they are revealed to us and accepted by faith, they remain concealed by the veil of faith itself and are, as it were, wrapped in darkness." Difficulties arise also from the historical condition that affects the expression of Revelation.
>
> With regard to this historical condition, it must first be observed that the meaning of the pronouncements of faith depends partly upon the expressive power of the language used at a given time and under given circumstances. Moreover, it sometimes happens that some dogmatic truth is first expressed incompletely (but not falsely), and at a later date, when considered in a broader context of faith or human knowledge, is expressed more fully and perfectly.[10]

The dynamic dimension of history had finally come to the fore within the Church. Language, meaning, values and cultures were seen as subject to change. This history of the human race was not the static record it was once thought to be. There was movement; there was change. Newman's *Development of Doctrine,* first published during the Victorian Age, had finally received official ecclesiastical approbation.

Besides giving their attention to these various aspects of history itself, many people were developing a greater awareness of "historical consciousness." Slowly they began to realize that they were not simply the pawns of forces that were totally beyond their control. Though the freedom they enjoyed was relative, not absolute, still they were able to create much of their own future by the various choices and decisions they made. Whatever those choices and decisions might be, others should respect them. Pluralism was becoming a constitutive element of society.

This pluralism had a definite effect on theology and was responsible for a decline in "common meaning." Edward Braxton defines this expression well when he writes that "common meaning exists when the interlocking elements of experiences, understandings, judgments and commitments are shared in a cohesive manner by members of a group."[11] In former times there had been general agreement among Catholics with regard to the meaning conveyed by much of our theological language. Whenever words such as God, Christ, sacrament, priesthood, etc., were employed, there was a common understanding as to what was meant by these terms. Now, these same words began to convey different meanings to different people because they no longer understood these words by reason of their common experiences, common understandings, common judgments and common commitments. On this very point, Braxton remarks that "so far-ranging is this pluralism that the actual formal belief of some Catholic people concerning a particular controversial doctrine may be closer to that of Christians of other traditions than it is to the 'official' Catholic position."[12]

A grace-filled exercise in self-understanding, the Second Vatican Council, instead of combatting this pluralism, actually fostered it. Many of the changes in thought and practice within the Church stem, at least in part, from the documents that represent the fruit of the Council's work and from the various movements it spawned. The new emphasis on freedom of conscience, the new understanding of the Church as the People of God, the new approach to other Christians and non-believers were ideas developed by Vatican II that were readily accepted by many, but rejected by others. Uniformity of thought among Catholics was giving way to diversity. This is not to say that the documents and movements appeared suddenly out of nowhere. Such theologians as John Courtney Murray, Karl Rahner, Henri de Lubac, Yves Congar, among others, who had a great deal of influence on the Council Fathers, had been writing and teaching along these lines for a number of years. Also, we must keep in mind that the Liturgical Movement had been moving forward in Europe and in the United States for several decades before the Council.

In his opening address to the Council, Pope John XXIII had pointed out the direction the Council should take. At that moment in the Church's history, all were required to read the "signs of the time" and to search for ways to bring the Church into ever closer contact with the world as it is. The Church could no longer afford to take an adversarial role vis-à-vis the world, but had to become its partner.

The Constitution on the Church in the Modern World best reflects the Council's effort to comply with the Pope's directive. In this document greater stress was placed on the Church's responsibility to make its presence felt in the real world, to challenge many of the world's values and to promote justice and peace everywhere. No longer would the Church be content with placing its emphasis on its internal structures.

More attention was paid by the Council to the role of the laity in the Church than to the role of the clergy. *The Constitution on the Liturgy* and the *Constitution on the Church*, as well as the *Decree on Bishops* did devote some of their statements to the role of the priest in the Church. Their treatment of the priesthood was quite traditional and contained little that was new. Some ideas long in the background did come to the fore, e.g., the priest as a member of a college, the priest as co-worker with the bishop. Perhaps not wishing to slight the clergy, the Council Fathers approved the *Decree on the Ministry and Life of Priests*. The title that they finally agreed upon gives some indication of the fact that they perceived ministry to have a certain priority. Though the cultic role of priests was deemed important, other roles were highlighted as well. The Proclamation of the Gospel was seen as the primary function of the priest; he was seen in relationship to others; ministry was viewed as their primary source of holiness; as leaders within the believing community, the priests were to awaken people's faith and form community. An issue that was not dealt with at all was the issue of celibacy. The document simply gives a stronger motivation by reminding priests that they have been consecrated to Christ and thus freed solely for the service of God.

Perhaps because of the decline of common meaning to which reference was made above, the reaction to the Council was varied. Those who were looking for changes in the Church saw the Council as a hopeful sign; those who wished to preserve the "status quo" saw it as a hopeless disaster. In 1970, John W. O'Malley, S.J. wrote an article in *Theological Studies* that was quite favorable toward Vatican II.[13] Nevertheless, he complains about the "turbulence" it created, about the "upheaval" it caused among religious and priests. One complaint he has is that the Council failed to tell us *how* we were to implement the goals it advocated. Such a reaction reflects the traditional understanding of the institutional church's role—to provide us with specific programs. Working through a process was seen as something that created too many problems. Yet, the Council Fathers were wise to use this latter approach, since it is more in keeping with the present understanding of the role the Church has in our lives. Perhaps O'Malley's somewhat "revolutionary" characterization of the Council was due to the fact that only a few years had elapsed since the end of the Council. Now, more than twenty years after the Council, its effects do not appear to be quite so radical. The use of the vernacular in the liturgy, the participation of the laity in a variety of ministries, the many pilgrimages of Pope Paul VI and John Paul II, the decline in resignations—all of these and other factors, especially the passage of time, have enabled people to see the Council from a different perspective.

All four factors—openness to change, the development of a sense of history and historical consciousness, the decline of common meaning, and the Second Vatican Council—contributed to a shift in emphasis as far as the teaching of religion in high schools and colleges and the teaching of theology in seminaries were concerned. The purely rational approach gave way to an experiential approach. Before one could offer any rational proofs for the existence of God, one had to reflect on the ordinary experiences of human life and find God there. Reflection on these experiences served as the foundation for any further development of one's faith.

It should surprise no one that such a method created a number of problems for those who viewed Christian life in this way for the first time. They began to experience a number of difficulties in relating to the God of their youth. They found little satisfaction in the prayer life to which they had become so accustomed. They could not blindly accept doctrines which came "from without" through ecclesial "revelations," but which had no relation to their human experience. They were unable to look upon their moral life as only a matter of total obedience to an extrinsic lawgiver who had established a code of conduct centuries earlier that was applicable for all times and in all situations. Finally, they found unacceptable the traditional doctrine of Divine Providence according to which their lives were programmed and evil existed only with God's permission.[14] They were confident, however, that a better understanding of the current teaching concerning God and Jesus Christ would assist them in their struggle to integrate their religious beliefs with their lives.

Nowhere in theology was a shift in emphasis more pronounced than with regard to the understanding of God and Jesus Christ, and this understanding affected every other theological discipline. Turning away from an excessive concentration on God's transcendence, theologians of the present era pay more attention to the reality of God's immanence. The story of the life, death and resurrection of Jesus is seen today as essentially a proclamation of the fact that God has been, is and always will be redemptively involved in human life and experience. God is not only for us; he is also with us and within us through His Spirit. And through this Spirit, God reveals himself to us in the multiple experiences of our lives in this world. That act of self-revelation has been happening since the human race began; it reached its fullness in Jesus Christ and continues to this day and into the future through the activity of God's Spirit which touches each of us in the most intimate and personal ways that we could possibly imagine. There is no need for us to conduct a search for God. He has already found us; he resides within the deepest recesses of our being. It is *there* he is to be found first and foremost.

To say all this is not to deny God's transcendence. We must continue to affirm that He is ineffable, incomprehensible—THE MYSTERY. But for people today, THE MYSTERY, while remaining mystery, has drawn nearer because we are so much more aware of His presence, His activity in the world and in us.

This contemporary awareness of a God who has drawn nearer to us has affected the way in which we perceive Jesus himself. We no longer, in the first place and primarily, concentrate on his Divinity, but we find our attention drawn to him as "one like us in all things but sin."

With regard to Christology, Donald F. Gray captures the mood of the present era when he writes:

> The classical christology of the Christian Church found expression in the metaphysical categories of nature and person. Today these categories are widely criticized as being too static and abstract, remnants of another and outmoded cultural era. A search for more dynamic and concrete categories, in keeping with the historical, processive, and inter-personal emphasis of modern thought, has been going on now for several decades and shows no signs of abating at present. We seem to be moving towards a formulation of the Church's christological convictions more in terms of activities rather than natures. Hopefully, such a formulation will serve not only to set out the faith of the community in a contemporary dress, but will also bring new insight into the meaning of the biblical depiction of Jesus as the Christ. One of the indispensable tasks of any such formulation will surely have to be a convincing vindication of the thoroughgoing humanness of Jesus, a humanness which the classical christology formally and officially defended, but practically and effectively undermined.[15]

Such an approach as Gray describes is still going on. No longer do we examine the life of Jesus and see there only the extraordinary, but rather the extraordinary in the ordinary. The Incarnation is no longer looked upon as a single event that fully occurred in a brief moment of time, but it is seen as a process that took place throughout Jesus' life, death and resurrection. Jesus, in his life, death and resurrection, is seen as the perfect manifestation of God's self-communication.

Because God is love and love is diffusive of itself, this self-communicating activity of God has taken place from the beginning of time. The history of God's chosen people, as found in the Old Testament, reflects that self-communication. In one member of that race it reached its ultimate historical manifestation because Jesus received that self-communication totally and responded to it fully. The evidence for this lies in the fact that in his public ministry he constantly sought to give to others what he himself had received. His openness to others, his concern for others, his obedient acceptance of all that happened to him, even his suffering and death—all of these were meant to serve as a model for each one of us. Jesus not only accomplished our salvation; he also taught us how to live.

We have come to realize that God's relationship to Jesus was essentially the same as God's relationship to us. To Jesus God has given Himself totally and Jesus responded to that gift fully. But to each of us also He truly continues to give Himself in the Spirit, thus enabling us also to respond to Him. Since Jesus truly possesses the same human nature we have, a real sense of identification with him is realizable. This master can truly be imitated by his disciples, for he first walked our way as one of us. Because he walked it perfectly, he and only he, is Lord and Son.

As a consequence of this view of God and Jesus, based on immanence rather than primarily on transcendence, there occurred a shift in the understanding of Grace, the Bible and the Church. Grace, instead of being viewed as a "thing" outside of us which was injected, especially through the Sacraments, has come to be perceived as God's Spirit-Life already within us. The Sacraments are seen now more as those sacred moments when we celebrate our conscious response to the Spirit-Life in a special way. The Bible, instead of being viewed as God's word spoken literally, has come to be understood as the response of the sacred writers to the Word-Activity (DABAR) of God in their lives. Though revelation, in the narrow sense, ended with the death of Saint John, revelation, in the broad sense, continues to occur in the daily lives of each of us because God's Word-Activity never ceases to invite our personal response. Finally, the Church, instead of being viewed primarily as an institutional structure, has come to be understood as the People of God gathered in communities, a sign of Christ's presence in the world, under the leadership of those who possess, not an authority based on power, but an authority based on service.

It should surprise no one that such shifts in theology as we have been describing had their effect on people's perception of priests. This is not to say that the laity necessarily had any direct contact with the "new theology." In many cases, the changes they experienced in this regard resulted more from the changes that were going on in society, e.g., the role of women, greater self-understanding, the human rights movement, etc. As was noted in the first section of this paper, in former times people's perception of the clergy was related, at least in part, to the special status priests had within the believing community, to the awesome powers they possessed and to the spiritual authority they exercised. Now things appear to be changing.

No longer do many Catholics depend on the clergy for help and advice as their parents and grandparents did. Catholics have made their way into the mainstream of American life. In politics, in industry, in almost any area where power and influence are exercised, Catholics can be found. Many of them are graduates of prestigious colleges and universities, Catholic or secular. They have left the ghettos of large cities to others and have moved to the suburbs or even out into the countryside. Many have climbed the corporate ladder in the business world, have achieved success in various professions, or have done well in the trades. If anything, the roles of the clergy and the laity have been reversed—now, the clergy look to the laity for assistance, particularly to those who have specialized in one or another occupation or profession.

Today, the awe that an older generation had associated with the special powers these priests possess is now expended on the marvelous inventions and accomplishments which human ingenuity has created over the last twenty years, e.g., computers. The atomic power of the forties and fifties has given way to the power of the megaton bombs. Space probes that eventually put a man on the moon have resulted in space satellites and space stations. There are so many marvels in the physical, visible world around us which demand our attention and respect that it should surprise no one that there is little awe left for the "awesome powers" that priests were believed to possess.

No longer do many Catholics look outside of themselves for authoritative sources. Better educated, surrounded by information available to them on all sides, feeling comfortable about looking to their own life experiences as a primary source in decision-making, they rely on their own conscience as their ultimate criterion. No longer do they rely on the clergy to make their decisions for them. Now, they are ready and willing to assume full responsibility here and in the hereafter for the decisions they make.

Most people have come to understand that priests are human, as they themselves are human; that priests are like them in all things, including sin. One of the factors that has contributed greatly to the improved relationship between priests and people is the increased involvement of the laity in matters ecclesial. Their roles in the liturgy as Ministers of the Word and Eucharist, their membership on parish councils, their work as catechists, their involvement in parish finances have brought them into closer contact with the clergy. They have come to recognize that, though priests have different roles or functions within the Church, the clergy still share with them the same human nature.

Without an objective analysis of the attitudes of a specific group of priests, the subject matter of the next chapter of this paper, it is perhaps somewhat presumptuous of me to offer any elaboration of the topic of priests' perception of themselves. Even with such an analysis, one must bear in mind that total uniformity of opinion cannot be expected. Pluriformity of ideas exists with regard to priesthood as well as other areas. The following observations have, therefore, a personal and subjective dimension to them and should be considered in that light.

Drawing on some of the ideas that I have developed above, I would now like to consider priests' perception of themselves in this period of tension and transition in terms of the history of the priesthood, the identity crisis that many priests are experiencing, the multiple role-expectations people put on them, and, finally, the issue of celibacy as an integral part of priesthood.

Before 1950, there was almost universal agreement among the general Catholic population with regard to a definition of the Sacrament of Holy Orders. One of the seven Sacraments, it was instituted by Jesus at the Last Supper, imprints an "indelible mark" on the soul of a baptized, male Catholic and bestows on him the power to forgive sins and to change bread and wine into the Body and Blood of Christ.

For centuries no strong evidence has surfaced to refute this notion. And there is none to this day. However, the giant strides that have been taken in our understanding of the New Testament have thrown new light on this particular subject. As a result, other possibilities have come to the fore. Nathan Mitchell, in his book *Mission and Ministry,* has offered an overview of the contemporary outlook which stresses the developmental nature of this particular Sacrament.[16] Permit me to summarize his assessment of this new approach to the Sacrament of Holy Orders.

Jesus undertook to establish a new movement within the Jewish faith, not a new religion. After his death and resurrection, his closest followers experienced his presence among them in an extraordinary way and came to believe that he had truly risen from the dead. This was the message they began to preach and soon they attracted a large following. Only gradually did they begin to disassociate themselves from the Jewish Temple and the synagogues. Prophets and evangelists joined them in spreading the Good News. The destruction of Jerusalem in 70 A.D. helped them to realize that they were establishing a new religion, that they were the "New Israel."

With the death of the last of the Apostles, the Christian community became aware of the fact that a serious problem confronted them. How would they preserve the authentic tradition concerning Jesus? The Matthaean solution was to depend on those who had assumed the teacher-scribe role within their communities. The Johannine alternative was to rely, not on people, but on the Paraclete.

In the meantime, perhaps in view of their ties to Judaism, the different Christian communities had established in their particular locales groups of "elders" called presbyters. They were not necessarily old in the chronological sense, but they were those who had been members of the Christian community for some length of time and had been living very exemplary lives. From this group were chosen the bishops who were charged with the duty of preserving the tradition, taking care of the community's finances and serving the needs of the community. For this latter function deacons were selected from among the elders to assist the bishops. As the number of Christians continued to multiply, the bishops saw the need to provide each of the local communities with leaders who would be their representatives. These leaders were the first priests, as we understand that term today. One of their most important duties was to preside at Eucharist as the bishop's representative.

In the earliest days of Christianity, Eucharist had been celebrated by the heads of households in whose homes the celebrations would occur. Gradually, since these early Christians saw themselves as belonging to a new religion and every religion needed a sacrifice, the sacrificial aspect of the Eucharist came to be emphasized. Bishops, considered to be the "high priests" of their newly founded religion, took over the role of Eucharistic leader. Later, as the need arose, priests assumed this role.

The idea that succession, in the literal sense, cannot be applied to the relationship between the Twelve Apostles and the bishops of today, as well as the idea that priesthood as we know it, may have had its origins, not in the time of Jesus or his apostles, but in the early second century or later, may cause many priests some uneasiness. Such uneasiness may be lessened, to some degree at least, by the realization that the Holy Spirit has been directly involved in this development. The exact moment of that involvement is of no great consequence.

Today many people in all walks of life find themselves experiencing an identity crisis. It should not surprise anyone that some priests find themselves in that very same situation. A possible source of the problem could be the dissatisfaction they feel in identifying who they are with what they do. In the case of the clergy, a great deal of attention is given to the functions they perform, functions that are highlighted in the definition of priesthood and in the Rite of Ordination itself. Perhaps, as a result of this, many priests have come to identify their priesthood with their functions. With this they are dissatisfied. Until they see priesthood as more than a function, until they realize that priesthood has more to do with who they are than what they do, this situation will continue.

The question, then, is not what does a priest do, but rather, who a priest is? In my view, a priest is someone who by reason of his particular life-experiences has become the person he is. Having been touched by the Spirit in a special way through Baptism, his life has followed a specific pattern. He spent several years of preparation in the seminary; he studied Philosophy and Theology, as well as other related disciplines; he has, hopefully, mastered the special skills needed for preaching, counseling and leading the faith community. Because he has become the person he now is, the Church officially commissions him in the Rite of Ordination to be its public representative and undertake a leadership role within the faith community. In that respect, he has become a "symbol of the Friendly Mystery." Given the Copernican revolution of Kant, as developed by cultural phenomenology, we realize today that all reality is symbolic, that is, it is psycho-socially constituted by patterns of meaning. The priest is a sacred or religious symbol because he, as priest, is constituted psycho-socially by patterns of religious meaning. His meaning, and hence reality, is "projected upon him" by the ecclesial community. In this way the priest becomes for the community a privileged and public symbol of God who, though utterly transcendent and complete within Himself, nonetheless lovingly gives Himself to all human beings. A priest's acceptance of himself in this dimension of his being, his recognition that such an awesome charism is his, can lessen the identity crisis he may find himself undergoing at the present time.[17]

The definition of the Sacrament of Holy Orders given earlier concentrates on the power associated with priesthood. Though it is readily acknowledged that this power is not given to the priest personally but that it is a power that is exercised for the good of the believing community, still this emphasis on power has made us lose sight of another aspect of priesthood on which the early church put great stress—the leadership a priest is called upon to exercise for the building up of the faith community.[18] Since so many expectations are being put on priests at the present time, it is perhaps propitious that this particular quality is one of which we are now more conscious. Besides being a man of prayer, a priest is expected to be a good preacher, a fine administrator, a resource person, a fund raiser—in short, he is expected to be "all things to all men"—and women too.

Given the fact that so much is expected of them, it is no wonder that some priests feel frustrated. If they possess even some of these abilities, well and good. Their main focus, however, should be on the leadership role that has been theirs, at least in theory, since the early days of the Christian era. Enabling people to discover the charism the Lord has given each of them for the building up of the faith community, as well as presiding at Eucharist, should be seen as their primary responsibility. Call them coordinators, energizers, animators or what you will, their special service to the community is to be found in this area. Like John the Baptizer, who pointed to Jesus and said "Behold the Lamb of God, behold him who takes away the sin of the world," priests are called to be the heralds of God's presence in every person and in the world around us. No longer can they be content to care only for those who are their immediate responsibility. They must be willing to reach out to the larger community. Working for peace and justice has long been considered the preserve of those who had a particular bent in that direction. Not so any more. For priests, as for the rest of the believing community, social justice is "a constitutive dimension of the preaching of the Gospel, or, in other words, of the Church's mission for the redemption of the human race and its liberation from every oppressive situation."[19] Being directly involved in the lives of people and serving their real needs in the world may be the means whereby priests' sense of frustration will decrease and their sense of fulfillment increase.

Despite the continuous stream of official pronouncements from the official magisterium, the question of priestly celibacy seems to remain an issue that just will not go away. Although it may well be that this was not a major consideration on the part of those who have resigned from priestly ministry over the course of the past twenty years, still the fact remains that for many of the priests today the lack of options in this matter is a cause for some anxiety.

There has been a universal law of celibacy for priests within the Roman Church since the twelfth century. Until recent times this law was accepted as a fact of life. Viewed as a requirement the Church imposed on those who aspired to priestly ordination, priests promised to observe celibacy, and, for the most part, they have been faithful to that promise.

Today, however, some priests fail to see celibacy as an integral part of priesthood for a number of reasons. More aware of the historical development of this particular law, they question its validity. Among them is Hans-Jurgen Vogels, who is the author of a *Concilium* article entitled "The Community's Right to a Priest in Collision with Compulsory Celibacy."[20] In this article Vogels attempts to show, through the exegesis of certain biblical texts which have been traditionally considered to endorse priestly celibacy, that this law has no validity. To further strengthen his argument, he cites certain New Testament data and makes much of the fact that the law came into existence so late in the Church's history.

In recent times the Church, perhaps aware that a legalistic approach to the matter of celibacy does not carry sufficient weight, has stressed the view that celibacy is to be considered a charism. Instead of resolving the issue, this approach would seem to have exacerbated the matter further. Vogels' comment on this aspect of the question is worth noting:

> The Second Vatican Council for the first time stressed the necessity of the charism, but at the same time 'confirmed' the 'law' which 'imposed' celibacy on all who were to be ordained. The council thereby forced all priests to keep the law, if necessary without the charism, which, according to Matt. 19:11 and I Cor.7:7, is not possible, or alternatively it wants, in the face of the New Testament statements that call married people to the priesthood, to compel God by a law to give all priests the charism of celibacy. God, however, who 'apportions to each one individually as he wills,' (I Cor. 12:11 RSV), cannot be compelled, even by prayer, for which the council calls, particularly since the possibility of obtaining the charism by prayer is very doubtful.[21]

In recent times priests have been urged to embrace celibacy "for the sake of the Kingdom," because its value as a sign of the Kingdom is most important for the good of the Church. One must keep in mind, however, that signs get their value from those who apply meaning to the signs. Just because the Council proclaims that there is a certain meaning attached to a particular sign does not mean that the people project that meaning on the sign. A meaning-less "sign" is no sign at all.

What can priests do? If they possess this gift or if they are content to remind others of the sign value of celibacy, they can rejoice. If not, they can continue their struggle to live out their commitment, hoping that, if not for themselves then for others, the day will come when this "heavy burden" will be lifted from their shoulders and that optional celibacy will be the rule and not the exception for priests of the Roman Catholic Church. There is also a third alternative regarding celibacy—priests can leave. This is a realistic possibility that must be acknowledged.

Thus far, we have been examining some of the traditional and contemporary views that many American priests and people have with regard to priesthood. This study would be incomplete if consideration were not given to Pope John Paul II's understanding of priesthood.

Much of his thinking on this subject is reflected in the speeches he has given and in the letters he has written over the course of these past five years of his pontificate. One becomes aware immediately of the strong emphasis he places on the Eucharist. This is certainly understandable in view of the important relationship that exists between priesthood and Eucharist. Moreover, one must bear in mind that during his travels to different countries he spoke very frequently to priests in the context of Eucharistic celebrations. Also, one cannot overlook the fact that Holy Thursday has been the occasion each year that he has chosen to send a message to priests throughout the world.

Given the understanding of priesthood today, it is somewhat surprising to find Pope John Paul II, in his letter to priests for Holy Thursday of 1983, expressing such ideas as the following:

> As we know, this day reminds us of the day on which, together with the Eucharist, the ministerial priesthood was instituted by Christ. The priesthood was instituted for the Eucharist and therefore for the church, which as the community of the people of God, is formed by the Eucharist. This priesthood, ministerial and hierarchical, is shared by us. We received it on the day of our ordination through the ministry of the bishop who transmitted to each one of us the sacrament begun with the apostles—begun at the Last Supper in the Upper Room on Holy Thursday.[22]

In the first such letter he composed in 1979, Pope John Paul made a similar reference. In the letter he also made use of much of the traditional language used in reference to priesthood. He wrote:

> The priesthood in which we share through the sacrament of orders, which has been forever "imprinted" on our souls through a special sign from God, that is to say the "character," remains in explicit relationship with the common priesthood of the faithful, that is to say the priesthood of all the baptized, but at the same time it differs from that priesthood "essentially and not only in degree."[23]

Toward the end of this same letter, he makes it quite clear that he does not believe that a Christian community has an intrinsic right to the Eucharist. To show priests how important their role in the Church is, he paints a poignant picture of a priestless community. The implication is that the situation can and will never change until such time as a priest validly ordained by a bishop comes into their midst.

There are, to be sure, faint echoes of some of the more recent ideas about priesthood to be found in his thinking. For example, in speaking to the priests in Nicaragua, the Pope referred to their role as animators when he said: "What joy the minister of Christ can experience as he sees a mature community forming about him and the various ministries of catechesis, charity and promotion arising out of it."[24] In the same address, however, he reminds them of what he had said to the priests in Mexico—that they are not social directors, political leaders or officials of temporal power. He seems to see priests as secondary movers, rather than primary, in the struggle for social justice. It would appear that, because of his position as Supreme Pontiff, he sees himself as the exception to the rule.

Given the Pope's Polish experience and given the fact that he has in many ways manifested a strong conservative stance during these years of his pontificate, one can readily opine that John Paul II's perception of priests and priesthood could be characterized as quite traditional. If one grants this, then it is safe to say that it is very doubtful that any significant changes "from above" will occur with regard to priests and priesthood. If any do take place, those changes will take place "from below." One does not like to dwell on the possible effects of such an eventuality.

The reader will recall that I entitled this section "The Way We Are Becoming." From this one might get the impression that some sort of universal change is to be expected in the priesthood and people's perception of it. Such, of course, is not the case. There is the possibility that we may eventually come full circle. That, however, seems very unlikely since, with the advent of pluralism, things will never be the same again. There will always be at least three different groups of priests—those who hold to the traditional approach to priesthood and for whom the transcendence of God and the divinity of Christ will be of utmost importance and whose priesthood will reflect these values; those who put more stress on God's immanence and on Jesus' humanity and who will try to discern the "signs of the times" and remain open to new possibilities; and, finally, those who will be somewhere in the middle.

Hopefully, all in priestly ministry, be they traditional, contemporary or otherwise, will be able to agree with the sentiments expressed by Karl Rahner concerning priests and the priesthood of the present as well as the future. The quotation, though lengthy, may enable all sides to see the priesthood in its proper perspective. He concludes his article "Theological Reflections on the Priestly Image of Today and Tomorrow" with these remarks:

> As Christians we do not have to calculate what the future of the priesthood will be in a futurologist sense. We do not have to estimate its chances and adapt ourselves accordingly. We have to believe in this future unconditionally, and by this act of faith to shape this future precisely when it seems to be improbable. Here too, we need not be those who suffer the future, but rather those who create it. In a spirit of faith, prayer and selflessness we have to overcome any tendency to a bourgeois 'establishment' attitude toward our priesthood as though it was a means of earning a living. We have to be the sort of priests who in the boldness of faith seize upon the folly of the Cross. We have to be not hirelings but shepherds who hope against all hope. We have to give our allegiance to the scandal of the Cross of Christ, to have the patience to endure historical situations which are impenetrable to our gaze. We have in a real sense to see ourselves as servants of Christ, that Christ who, through the fathomless darkness of his death, has redeemed the world. We have to be ready to bear unemotionally and in all the realism of our colourless everyday lives the stigmata of Christ. And if we do all this then we are priests indeed, then it is the grace of God alone which is creating through us, and also through our priest-

hood, that future which the one and unique Lord of history and the Church has devised for this priesthood and which will come to pass.[25]

All that has been said in the course of this chapter should be seen as setting the stage for what is to follow. Subjective and somewhat speculative, the opinions put forth may be debated. In the next chapter I hope to achieve a certain degree of objectivity by ascertaining the views that a specific group of priests have with regard to priestly ministry.

Endnotes

[1]Thomas F. O'Meara, O.P., *Theology of Ministry* (New York/Ramsey: Paulist Press, 1983), pp. 124-125.

[2]Despite an intensive search, I was unable to find a scholarly reference for this quotation.

[3]Eugene F. Kennedy and Victor J. Heckler, *The Catholic Priest in the United States: Psychological Investigations* (Washington: USCC, 1972), pp. 5-6.

[4]James A. Mohler, S.J., *The Origin and Evolution of the Priesthood* (New York: Alba House, 1970), p. xiii.

[5]*Essays on the Priesthood* (St. Meinrad, Indiana: St. Meinrad's Press, 1954), p. 42.

[6]Ibid., p. 79.

[7]Ibid., p. 5.

[8]Gregory Baum, *Man Becoming* (New York: Herder and Herder, 1970), pp. 4-5.

[9]Ibid., pp. 33-34.

[10]*The Pope Speaks* (Washington: USCC, 1973), 18, no. 2, p. 151.

[11]Edward J. Braxton, *The Wisdom Community* (New York/Ramsey: Paulist Press, 1980), p. 40.

[12]Ibid., p. 41.

[13]John W. O'Malley, S.J., "Reform, Historical Consciousness and Vatican II's Aggiornamento," *Theological Studies* 32 (1971) p. 573.

[14]Gregory Baum, idem, pp. 163 ff.

[15]Donald F. Gray, "The Incarnation: God's Giving and Man's Receiving," *Horizons* 1 (1974), p. 1.

[16]Nathan Mitchell, O.S.B., *Mission and Ministry* (Wilmington, Delaware: Michael Glazier, 1982), pp. 140 ff.

[17]Ideas gleaned from class discussion with Sister Patricia Smith, R.S.M. and from conversations with Rev. Donald Buggert, O.Carm.

[18]Nathan Mitchell, O.S.B., idem., p. 303.

[19]III Synod of Bishops, *Justice in the World* (Washington: USCC, 1969), p. 34.

[20]Hans-Jurgen Vogels, "The Community's Right to a Priest in Collision with Compulsory Celibacy," in *Concilium 133 Right of the Community to a Priest,* eds. Edward Schillebeeck and J. Metz (New York: Seabury Press, 1980), pp. 84ff.

[21]Ibid., p. 90.

[22]John Paul II, "Holy Thursday 1983: Pope's Letter to Priests," *Origins* 12 (April 17, 1983): 688.

[23]John Paul II, "A Letter to Priests," *Origins* 8 (April 19, 1979): 697.

[24]John Paul II, "The Priest, the Man of Dialogue," Origins 12 (March 17, 1983): 641.

[25]Karl Rahner, "Theological Reflections on the Priestly Image of Today and Tomorrow," *Theological Investigations* 12, trans. David Bourke (London: Darton, Longman and Todd, 1974) pp. 59-60.

2.

Procedures and Methodology

Having provided some background material about the priesthood in the United States during this present century, I shall now move on to a discussion of the questionnaire administered to the priests associated with the Diocese of Joliet in 1984. Dr. Paul Kaiser, Director of Computer Programming, and Dr. Michael Reich, a member of the faculty in the Department of Psychology, both associated with Lewis University in Romeoville, Illinois, assisted me in the development of the questionnaire and assured me that the instrument could achieve its objective and provide a goodly amount of information concerning this group of priests. And their opinion was bolstered by that of Monsignor Colin MacDonald.

Joseph L. Imesch, D.D., Bishop of the Diocese of Joliet, had very graciously consented to write a cover letter which was sent out with the questionnaire. Both were sent out to three hundred and seventy-nine priests during the first week of May in 1984. After a ten day period had elapsed, a postcard, bearing the signature of Rev. Hugh Fullmer, Diocesan Director of Continuing Education, was to be sent out. This proved to be unnecessary, as within a two week period one hundred and ninety-seven were returned, with six arriving at a later date (too late to be fed into the computer). A few were rejected because they were only partially filled out. One responded with nothing but a cartoon.

The responses were fed into a computer by the students in one of Dr. Kaiser's classes at Lewis University. The information has finally been reported and does, I believe, reflect the thoughts and feelings of this group of priests with regard to their theology of priesthood, their ministerial practices, sources of stress, reasons for remaining active in the ministry and their attitude toward vocation recruitment. The various sections of the questionnaire together with a commentary and an analysis for each, follow.

Section I—Background Information

Instructions: Please complete the following statements or check the appropriate space.

1. I was born in 19___. (N-189)*

-1909	(5.8%)
1910-1919	(15.3%)
1920-1929	(16.4%)
1930-1939	(31.7%)

*Whenever it occurs, (N-) refers to the number of those who responded to a particular item.

1940-1949	(21.7%)
1950-1959	(9.0%)

2. I was ordained in 19__. (N-189)

-1934	(6.9%)
1935-1944	(12.7%)
1945-1954	(13.8%)
1955-1964	(27.0%)
1965-1974	(22.8%)
1975-	(16.9%)

3. I am a diocesan priest (56.8%) ; a religious order priest (43.2%) . (N-190)

4. I have been in my present assignment for __. (N-176)

0-3	years (47.2%)
4-6	years (23.9%)
7-9	years (9.7%)
10-14	years (10.2%)
15-19	years (5.7%)
20+	years (3.4%)

Note: For items 5-7, choose from the Response Categories listed below.

Response Categories

1. Full-time diocesan staff person

2. Pastor with special work outside the parish

3. Pastor without special work outside the parish

4. Associate Pastor with special work outside the parish

5. Associate Pastor without special work outside the parish

6. Priest in special ministry

7. Full-time teacher

8. Priest in retirement

9. Other (Please describe) _____

5. #____best describes my present assignment.(N-187)

#1 (3.7%)	#4 (8.0%)	#7 (6.4%)
#2 (11.8%)	#5 (17.6%)	#8 (5.9%)
#3 (21.4%)	#6 (18.7%)	#9 (6.4%)

6. #____best describes the nature of the assignment I had before my present one. (If this is your first assignment, please leave the space blank). (N-166)

#1 (4.2%)	#4 (9.0%)	#7 (9.2%)
#2 (12.0%)	#5 (28.3%)	#8 (0.6%)
#3 (15.7%)	#6 (12.0%)	#9 (7.8%)

7. #____has been or would be the most fulfilling for me. (N-174)

#1 (4.6%)	#4 (9.2%)	#7 (9.2%)
#2 (12.6%)	#5 (10.9%)	#8 (1.7%)
#3 (29.3%)	#6 (18.4%)	#9 (4.0%)

8. Of the following categories, #____best describes the type of community in which I am presently serving. (N-185)

1) Urban   2) Suburban   3) Rural   4) Other____
(17.3%)   (56.2%)   (12.4%)   (14.1%)

9. Of the following categories, #____best describes the time of my entrance into the seminary. (N-189)

1) after grammar school (34.9%)
2) during high school (9.0%)
3) just after finishing high school (16.4%)
4) after high school, some working experience and/or some advanced study (23.8%)
5) after completing college (6.9%)
6) after college and some working experience (5.8%)
7) after obtaining a higher degree and some working experience (3.2%)

10. Of the following statements, #____best describes my emotional state. (N-188)

1) I have the usual emotional "ups and downs" of an adult. (79.3%)
2) Occasionally I have problems of emotional tension or discouragement. (18.6%)
3) I have extended periods of emotional disturbance or discouragement. (1.1%)
4) I have emotional problems serious enough to prevent me from carrying out my duties to the best of my ability. (1.1%)

11. Of the following categories, #____best describes my heritage.
(N-189)

1)Polish-American (9.0%)	4)Black-American (0.5%)	7)Slavic-American (8.5%)
2)Irish-American (24.9%)	5)Hispanic-American (0.0%)	8)Mixed Heritage (16.4%)
3)German-American (16.9%)	6)Italian-American (11.1%)	9)Other (describe) (12.7%)

12. Of the following adverbs, #____best describes how well I think my training prepared me for the responsibilities of priesthood. (N-189)

1) very well (33.3%)
2) well (34.9%)
3) adequately (25.4%)
4) poorly (5.8%)
5) very poorly (0.5%)

13. I have given the thought of leaving the priesthood serious consideration. (Please check one) (N-187)

1) __never (68.4%)

2) __occasionally (30.5%)

3) __frequently (1.1%)

Note: If you check #2 or #3 above, please indicate if any of the following reflect your thinking.

14. Sometimes I think I would like to leave, but I fear that I might not adjust easily to life outside the priesthood. (N-44)

YES (25.0%)   NO (75.0%)

2) I would like to leave, but I would be afraid of going against God's Will. (N-43)

YES (23.3%)   NO (76.7%)

3) I would like to leave, but I do not think that I would be happy if I did. (N-45)

YES (35.6%)   NO (64.4%)

4) I would like to leave, but I could not handle the pressure from peers, family and friends. (N-43)

YES (23.3%)   NO (76.7%)

Commentary

The majority of the respondents (69.2%) were born in the period prior to World War II. 21.7% saw the light of day during the forties and the remaining 9% in the fifties. With regard to the year of ordination, the majority (60.4%) received the Sacrament of Holy Orders prior to the promulgation of the documents of the Second Vatican Council. Although the number of diocesan priests and religious order priests working in the diocese is about even, the number of diocesan priests (56.8%) who responded was greater than the number of religious order priests (43.2%).

With regard to the length of time the priests have been in their present assignment, the majority (71.1%) have been there for six years or less. Those assignments cover a wide range of ministries with slightly more than half involved in parish ministry as pastors or associate pastor (58.8%). It is interesting to note that there are fewer associate pastors now (17.6%) than previously (28.3%) and more priests involved in special ministry now (18.7%) than before (12%). The number of priests in retirement went from .6% to 5.9%, in terms of present as compared with previous assignments, and of the eleven who make up the latter category only three would appear to be happy with their lot. Pastors with special work outside the parish (11.8%) seem to be quite content. Of all the possible assignments, those that have been or would be most fulfilling are: pastor without special work outside the parish (29.3%) and priest in special ministry (18.4%) Finally, it is quite evident that the majority (73.5%) of the priests work in the cities or the suburbs of the Diocese of Joliet.

Let us consider now some other aspects of the background of the priests who responded to the questionnaire. They were asked to provide some information concerning the time of their entrance into the seminary, their present emotional state, their ethnic heritage, and an evaluation of their seminary training. Finally, they were asked to indicate if they had ever seriously considered leaving the active ministry and if any of the reasons cited applied to them.

43.9% of the respondents were products of minor seminary training, with 16.4% entering after the completion of four years of high school. Another 23.8% entered after high school with some working experience and/or some advanced study. The remaining 15.9% entered the seminary after college. With regard to the evaluation of their seminary training in terms of preparing them for the responsibilities of priesthood, 68.2% were quite satisfied, 25.4% considered the training adequate and the remaining 6.3% were of the opinion that they were poorly prepared. As to their emotional state at the time they filled out the questionnaire, 79.3% saw themselves as having the usual emotional "ups and downs" of adults. 18.6% felt that they had some problems of emotional tension or discouragement, and the remaining 11.1% felt that their problems were of a more serious nature.

As far as ethnic heritage is concerned, the largest percentage (24.9) had an Irish-American background 16.9% considered themselves to be German-American, 11.1% Italian-American, 9.0% Polish-American, 8.5% Slavic-American, and the remaining 29.1% were of a mixed or "other" heritage. It is interesting to note that none claimed an Hispanic heritage and only .5% were Black-American.

Finally, with regard to the issue as to whether or not they had given the thought of leaving the priesthood serious consideration, 68.4% of the respondents answered negatively, 30.5% admitted that they had occasionally and 1.1% thought about it frequently. Of the forty or so who responded to the possible reasons cited, 25% felt that they could not adjust easily to life outside the priesthood, 23.3% were afraid that they would be going against God's will, 35.6% did not think they would be happy if they left and 23.3% believed that they would not be able to handle the pressure from peers, family and friends.

Analysis

From what I have seen and read, I believe it is safe to say that, in most respects, the respondents to the questionnaire are quite representative of the priests in the Diocese of Joliet and, in fact, of the priests throughout the United States—at least in terms of much of the demographic information that has been obtained in the course of my research. The fact that such a large majority were born prior to World War II means that the "graying of America" has reached down into the presbyterate of the Diocese of Joliet. In a few years time the majority of the priests will have celebrated their Silver Jubilee of ordination. Since the number of priests ordained the past several years is rather small, all of this means that, unless a miracle of some sort occurs, there will be a crisis with regard to "priest power" within the diocese.

In the commentary, reference was made to the fact that fewer religious order priests responded to the questionnaire as compared with diocesan priests. I do not believe that this means there was a lack of interest in the matter, so much as it may reflect the fact that they saw the questionnaire directed primarily to priests who were engaged in parochial ministry, and the majority of said religious order priests found themselves involved in other forms of pastoral ministry.

The fact that 71% of the priests have been in their present assignment for less than six years would seem to indicate that there is a good degree of mobility among the clergy. There are fewer associate pastors at the present time and more priests involved in special ministries. This would seem to suggest that the diocesan leadership and the priests themselves have come to realize that the parish setting is not the only place where the clergy can exercise ministry. Within the past few years priests have become involved in Family Life ministry and in ministry to the Hispanics, to mention just a few. Though the number of retired priests who responded was not very large, mention was made of the fact that only three of the eleven seemed to be content with their lot. To me, this means the level of discontent is quite high and some attention should be directed toward a solution.

Close to 50% of the priests began their studies for the priesthood on the minor seminary level. Today there seems to be a reluctance on the part of many to encourage young men to enter at such a young age. As a result, there are few minor seminaries in operation. Given the fact that few are ordained each year, greater attention will have to be paid to the vocation crisis.

The fact that the vast majority of the respondents felt that they had been well trained in the seminary or were quite satisfied with the training they received means that they feel capable of fulfilling their ministerial responsibilities. Since 79.3% saw themselves as having the usual emotional "ups and downs" of adults, one can readily conclude that the priests are quite normal. As far as ethnic heritage is concerned, there seems to be quite a good mix. However, the fact that there are no priests with an Hispanic heritage and only one Black-American means that greater attention must be given to this situation, considering the large Hispanic and Black population in parts of the diocese.

Given the times in which we live, it should surprise no one that approximately 30% of the priests have given serious consideration, at least occasionally, to the idea of leaving the active ministry. Some of the respondents checked the possible reasons suggested in the questionnaire. Since, as we shall see in the next section, 45% do not consider celibacy to be an integral part of the priesthood, there is the possibility that this could have contributed to their thought process. I regret that I did not list this issue as a possible reason.

Section II—Theology of Priesthood

Instructions: Please circle the number on each line that comes closest to expressing your belief about the following statements.

4-Agree Strongly   3-Agree   2-Disagree   1-Disagree Strongly

1. Celibacy should be maintained as an integral part of priesthood in the Western Church. (N-189)

    4 (29.1%)   3 (25.9%)   2 (28.0)   1 (16.9%)

2. In presiding at Eucharist, the most important activity of the priest as mediator between God and humanity, is to unite himself with Jesus. (N-184)

    4 (40.8%)   3 (26.6%)   2 (25.0%)   1 (7.6%)

3. The ordination of women is an impossibility from a theological point of view. (N-186)

    4 (19.4%)   3 (14.0%)   2 (34.4%)   1 (32.3%)

4. The Proclamation of the Word is not confined to preaching from the pulpit. (N-189)

    4 (66.0%)   3 (30.4%)   2 (1.6%)   1 (1.0%)

5. Priesthood has more to do with who a priest is than what he does. (N-184)

    4 (38.7%)   3 (30.9%)   2 (21.5%)   1 (5.2%)

6. Clergy who have married should be permitted to resume their priestly role within the Church. (N-186)

4 (25.8%)   3 (32.8%)   2 (29.6%)   1 (11.8%)

7. The priest at the Altar serves as the representative of the People of God rather than as their substitute. (N-180)

4 (54.4%)   3 (42.8%)   2 (2.2%)   1 (0.6%)

8. The characterization of priests who leave as being nothing more than other "Judases" is justified. (N-188)

4 (3.7%)   3 (2.1%)   2 (21.3%)   1 (72.9%)

9. The ordination of women is contrary to the will of Christ. (N-176)

4 (16.5%)   3 (17.0%)   2 (31.3%)   1 (35.2%)

10. The gift of celibacy is something that one receives from the Lord in response to earnest prayer. (N-182)

4 (16.5%)   3 (50.5%)   2 (22.5%)   1 (10.4%)

11. Priesthood is only one of many ministries within the Church. (N-187)

4 (51.9%)   3 (43.9%)   2 (3.2%)   1 (1.1%)

12. The leadership role of priests is best demonstrated in the administration of the Sacraments. (N-183)

4 (15.8%)   3 (41.5%)   2 (36.8%)   1 (6.0%)

13. Ordination confers on the priest a permanent character which makes him essentially different from the laity within the Church. (N-186)

4 (25.3%)   3 (38.2%)   2 (24.7%)   1 (11.8%)

14. The idea that the priest is a "man set apart" is a barrier to the full realization of true Christian community. (N-187)

4 (10.7%)   3 (26.7%)   2 (40.6%)   1 (21.9%)

15. With the new roles for everyone that have developed in the Church since Vatican II, the relationships between laity are much better. (N-182)

4 (18.1%)   3 (63.7%)   2 (13.2%)   1 (4.9%)

16. The term "presbyter" and the term "priest" have always been synonymous. (N-178)

4 (5.6%)   3 (33.7%)   2 (49.4%)   1 (11.2%)

17. Priesthood is primarily a function. (N-183)

4 (3.8%)   3 (16.9%)   2 (53.0%)   1 (26.2%)

18. Given the possibility, one could trace his priestly lineage through the bishop who ordained him, down through the centuries, back to the Apostles who were ordained by Jesus at the Last Supper. (N-177)

4 (23.7%)   3 (47.5%)   2 (22.6%)   1 (6.2%)

19. The chief reason for the restoration of the diaconate was to alleviate the shortage of priests. (N-185)

4 (5.4%)   3 (24.9%)   2 (49.7%)   1 (20.0%)

20. The term "priesthood of the faithful" is merely a figure of speech. (N-188)

4 (4.3%)   3 (5.9%)   2 (47.3%)   1 (42.6%)

Commentary

In the second section, dealing with the theology of priesthood, I composed twenty statements which I hoped would serve to reveal the attitude the respondents had with regard to certain aspects of this topic. I attempted to discover their views on celibacy, the ordination of women, inactive priests, the origin and nature of the Sacrament of Holy Orders and the ministerial role of the priest in terms of Word and Sacrament.

With regard to celibacy, 55% see it as an integral part of priesthood in the Western Church, while the other 45% do not consider it to be essential. A surprising 67% understand the gift of celibacy to be something one receives from the Lord in response to earnest prayer.

Although the respondents were not asked directly if they were for or against the ordination of women, it appears that at least 66.7% see it as something that is not an impossibility from a theological point of view and 66.5% do not consider it to be contrary to the will of Christ.

If they were to have their way, it would appear that 58.6% of the respondents would approve of the idea of having priests who left and married resume their priestly role within the Church. 94.2% do not believe that those who leave the active ministry should be characterized as "other Judases," and of this percentage 72.9% STRONGLY disagreed with the statement.

It was interesting to discover that 71.2% of the priests accept the idea that their priestly lineage can be traced back directly to the apostles. 63.5% subscribe to the traditional idea that ordination confers on the priest a permanent character which makes him essentially different from the laity. More than one third of the respondents

(39.3%) consider the terms "presbyter" and "priest" to be synonymous. 69.6% accept the idea that priesthood has more to do with who a person IS rather than what he DOES, but an even greater percentage (79.2%) do not consider priesthood to be primarily a function. 95.8% see priesthood as one of many ministries in the church and 81.8% believe that the relationship between clergy and laity has improved since Vatican II.

Only slightly more than half (57.3%) are of the opinion that the priest best exercises his leadership role in the administration of the Sacraments. 96.4% agreed that the Proclamation of the Word was not confined to preaching from the pulpit. It is worthy of note that 97.2% see the priest as the representative of the people of God, but 67.4% were of the opinion that, as presider, the priest's most important activity is to unite himself with Jesus. Finally, 69.7% understand that the restoration of the diaconate did not take place in order to alleviate the shortage of priests and 89.9% realize that the term "priesthood of the faithful" is much more than a figure of speech.

Analysis

Since only slightly more than half of the respondents believe that there is an essential relationship between priesthood and celibacy, this means that a goodly number of them do not. Also, those who do have a decidedly different point of view from a rather large percentage of the laity who, in recent polls, signified that they do not object to priests being married. I found the response to the statement about celibacy as a gift somewhat surprising because it would appear that many failed to appreciate the fact that, as gift or charism, celibacy is not the result of earnest prayer, but is actually pure gift.

The responses to statements concerning the ordination of women and the reinstatement of priests who have married indicate a fairly positive attitude toward these issues. The fact that they responded so strongly against the idea of labeling priests as "other Judases" shows that they bear no ill will toward those who have left the active ministry.

Apparently, a significant number of the respondents (71.2%) believe that the phrase "instituted by Christ" in the definition of a sacrament applies directly and immediately to the Sacrament of Holy Orders. The fact that some 40% consider priesthood and presbyterate to have always been synonymous supports this view and demonstrates that many of the respondents do not see any developmental element in the Sacrament of Holy Orders. That almost 40% rejected the traditional idea that ordination confers on a priest a permanent character which makes him essentially different from the laity may be due to the use of the words "essentially different." Since so many spurned the idea that ordination separated them from the laity, this could mean that they see their ROLE as essentially different, but not themselves. The very positive response to the statements concerning the priesthood as one of many ministries in the Church and concerning the better relationships between clergy and laity since Vatican II means that they see a greater unity within the Church than ever before.

Only slightly more than half (57.3%) point to the administration of the sacraments as the best exercise of their leadership role. This would seem to indicate that, for others, another role (prophet, "enabler"?) may be of primary importance.

I found a bit of a contradiction in the responses to the statement about the priest being God's representative at the altar and the statement about the priest's most important activity there. If 67.4% of the respondents saw the priest's most important activity to be union with Jesus, how could 97.2% subscribe to the idea that the priest is the representative of the people and not their substitute? It was encouraging to note that almost 70% of the respondents have some understanding that the diaconate was restored for a reason other than the alleviation of the priest shortage, and it was even more encouraging to see that almost 90% realize that the term "priesthood of the faithful" is much more than a figure of speech.

3.

Pastoral Practice

In the following two sections I have elected to make use of a slightly different approach. After presenting the raw data of the questionnaire, instead of doing a commentary and then an analysis immediately, I shall first give capsulized versions of each item, according to percentages with regard to importance and frequency. I have combined the "very important" and "important" responses, as well as the "very frequently" and "frequently" responses in order to simplify matters. The remaining percentage that is not shown for each of the items would, of course, refer to the responses that were found in the "somewhat important" or "not important" columns and the "infrequently" or "not at all" columns. Each display will be followed by a commentary and then an analysis.

Section III—Pastoral Practices

The following are some of the elements in the pastoral life of a priest that can be fulfilling and rewarding.

For each of the items use the numbers *to signify their importance in your life and the* letters *to signify their* frequency in your life.

4-Very important 3-Important 2-Somewhat important 1-Not important

A-Very frequently B-Frequently C-Infrequently D-Not at all

1. Visiting the sick.

(N-189)	4 (46.6%)	3 (39.7%)	2 (13.2%)	1 (0.5%)
(N-185)	A (24.3%)	B (48.6%)	C (26.5%)	D (0.5%)

2. Helping the poor people.

(N-187)	4 (40.1%)	3 (46.5%)	2 (12.8%)	1 (0.5%)
(N-183)	A (15.3%)	B (43.7%)	C (37.7%)	D (3.3%)

3. Participating in some significant social action such as a rally or a demonstration.

(N-186)	4 (2.7%)	3 (11.3%)	2 (49.5%)	1 (36.6%)
(N-183)	A (0.0%)	B (3.8%)	C (39.9%)	D (56.3%)

4. Supporting the causes of minorities.

(N-186)	4 (21.5%)	3 (50.0%)	2 (24.7%)	1 (3.8%)
(N-183)	A (7.1%)	B (25.7%)	C (49.7%)	D (17.5%)

5. Actively participating in small group discussions on spiritual concerns.

| (N-187) | 4 (26.2%) | 3 (51.3%) | 2 (17.6%) | 1 (4.8%) |
| (N-183) | A (12.0%) | B (49.2%) | C (32.2%) | D (6.6%) |

6. Doing some kind of work with the mentally ill or the retarded.

| (N-187) | 4 (9.1%) | 3 (34.2%) | 2 (41.2%) | 1 (15.5%) |
| (N-184) | A (4.3%) | B (10.3%) | C (46.7%) | D (38.6%) |

7. Working for better political leadership.

| (N-182) | 4 (7.1%) | 3 (30.2%) | 2 (39.0%) | 1 (23.6%) |
| (N-182) | A (2.2%) | B (6.6%) | C (42.9%) | D (48.4%) |

8. Providing recreational facilities for the young and disadvantaged.

| (N-186) | 4 (8.6%) | 3 (11.5%) | 2 (46.8%) | 1 (17.2%) |
| (N-183) | A (3.8%) | B (11.5%) | C (40.4%) | D (44.3%) |

9. Teaching in a Catholic institution.

| (N-188) | 4 (31.9%) | 3 (31.4%) | 2 (24.5%) | 1 (12.2%) |
| (N-184) | A (26.1%) | B (28.3%) | C (26.1%) | D (19.6%) |

10. Teaching in a non-Catholic institution.

| (N-184) | 4 (9.8%) | 3 (23.9%) | 2 (34.8%) | 1 (31.5%) |
| (N-182) | A (3.8%) | B (3.8%) | C (26.9%) | D (65.4%) |

11. Working for a social organization or a civil rights group.

| (N-186) | 4 (5.4%) | 3 (19.9%) | 2 (42.5%) | 1 (32.3%) |
| (N-183) | A (1.6%) | B (7.7%) | C (27.9%) | D (62.8%) |

12. Helping anti-nuclear or pro-peace groups.

| (N-188) | 4 (13.3%) | 3 (35.6%) | 2(35.1%) | 1 (16.0%) |
| (N-185) | A (2.2%) | B (16.8%) | C (40.5%) | D (40.5%) |

13. Helping the Right-to-Life movement.

| (N-188) | 4 (23.4%) | 3 (43.1%) | 2 (27.7%) | 1 (5.9%) |
| (N-184) | A (6.5%) | B (25.0%) | C (53.8%) | D (14.7%) |

14. Counseling people.

| (N-189) | 4 (59.8%) | 3 (33.9%) | 2 (6.3%) | 1 (0.0%) |
| (N-187) | A (44.9%) | B (46.5%) | C (8.0%) | D (0.5%) |

15. Administering the Sacraments.

| (N-187) | 4 (73.4%) | 3 (24.5%) | 2 (2.1%) | 1 (0.0%) |
| (N-186) | A (76.9%) | B (22.0%) | C (1.1%) | D (0.0%) |

16. Working with people to increase their faith awareness.

| (N-187) | 4 (70.1%) | 3 (27.3%) | 2 (2.7%) | 1 (0.0%) |
| (N-185) | A (50.3%) | B (41.1%) | C (7.6%) | D (1.1%) |

17. Presiding at Eucharistic celebrations.

| (N-188) | 4 (84.0%) | 3 (14.9%) | 2 (0.5%) | 1 (0.5%) |
| (N-185) | A (84.3%) | B (14.6%) | C (0.5%) | D (0.5%) |

18. Working with parish organizations.

| (N-190) | 4 (43.2%) | 3 (40.0%) | 2 (12.6%) | 1 (4.2%) |
| (N-188) | A (39.9%) | B (31.9%) | C (19.1%) | D (9.0%) |

19. Engaging in efforts to bring about social reforms on the local level.

| (N-187) | 4 (11.2%) | 3 (47.6%) | 2 (33.7%) | 1 (7.5%) |
| (N-188) | A (4.3%) | B (20.4%) | C (48.4%) | D (26.9%) |

20. Having the opportunity to work with people and to be a part of their lives.

| (N-188) | 4 (58.0%) | 3 (29.8%) | 2 (11.7%) | 1 (0.5%) |
| (N-185) | A (51.9%) | B (29.2%) | C (15.7%) | D (3.2%) |

21. Equipping lay groups to evangelize others.

| (N-188) | 4 (42.0%) | 3 (46.8%) | 2 (9.0%) | 1 (2.1%) |
| (N-185) | A (14.1%) | B (43.2%) | C (32.4%) | D (10.3%) |

22. Preaching.

| (N-190) | 4 (88.4%) | 3 (11.1%) | 2 (0.5%) | 1 (0.0%) |
| (N-188) | A (84.0%) | B (16.0%) | C (0.0%) | D (0.0%) |

Display
Importance of Pastoral Practice*

Preaching. (#22) 99.5%

Presiding at Eucharist. (17) 98.9%

Administering the Sacraments. (15) 97.9%

Help increase faith awareness. (16) 97.4%

Counseling. (14) 93.7%

Equipping laity to evangelize. (21) 88.8%

*Pastoral Practices ranked according to sum of responses: "Very important" and "Important."

Being part of people's lives. (20) 87.6%

Helping poor people. (2) 86.6%

Visiting the sick. (1) 86.3%

Working with parish groups. (18) 77.5%

Small group discussions. (5) 76.5%

Helping Right-to-Life movement. (13) 76.5%

Supporting minorities. (#4) 71.4%

Teaching in Catholic Schools. (9) 63.3%

Bring social reform locally. (19) 58.8%

Help anti-nuclear or peace groups. (12) 49.9%

Working with retarded. (6) 43.3%

Better political leadership. (7) 37.3%

Rec. facilities for young. (8) 36.0%

Teach in non-Catholic schools. (10) 33.7%

Social or civil rights groups. (11) 25.3%

Significant social action. (3) 14.0%

Display
Frequency of Pastoral Practice*

Frequency

Preaching. (#22) 100.0%

*Pastoral Practice ranked according to sum of responses: "Very frequently" and "Frequently."

Presiding at Eucharist. (17) 98.9%

Administering the Sacraments. (15) 98.9%

Helping increase faith awareness. (16) 91.4%

Counseling. (14) 91.4%

Being part of people's lives. (20) 81.1%

Visiting the sick. (1) 72.9%

Working with parish groups. (18) 71.8%

Small group discussions. (5) 61.2%

Helping poor people. (2) 59.0%

Equipping laity to evangelize. (21) 57.3%

Teaching in Catholic schools. (9) 54.4%

Supporting minorities. (4) 32.8%

Helping Right-to-Life movement. (13) 31.5%

Bring social reform locally. (19) 24.7%

Help anti-nuclear or peace groups. (12) 19.0%

Rec. facilities for young. (8) 15.3%

Working with the retarded. (6) 14.6%

Social or civil rights groups. (11) 9.3%

Better political leadership. (7) 8.8%

Teaching in non-Catholic school. (10) 7.6%

Significant social action. (3) 3.8%

Commentary

99.9% of the respondents consider preaching important to their ministry, and all of them see it as something they do very frequently. For 98.9% presiding at Eucharist is an important element of their ministry, and the same percentage do so frequently. 97.9% give importance to administering the Sacraments, and 98.9% find this something they do frequently. Helping people increase their faith awareness is important for 97.4%, and 91.4% of the respondents report that they do this frequently. Counseling is an activity that 93.7% of the priests consider important, and 91.4% indicate that they are so occupied frequently.

Equipping the laity with the means to evangelize is rated important by 88.8% of the priests, but only 57.3% report it as something they do frequently. For 87.6% it is important to be a part of people's lives, and 81.1% find themselves doing so frequently. 86.6% believe that helping the poor is a major activity for them, but only 59% indicate that they do this with any regularity. The same percentage (86.3%) consider visiting the sick an important element of their ministry, and 72.9% find time to do so with some frequency. Working with parish groups is important to 77.5% of the priests and is something that 71.8% find themselves engaged in quite regularly.

Both participating in small group discussions and helping the Right-to-Life Movement are important to 76.5% of the respondents, with 61.2% engaging in the former frequently, but only 31.5% involved in the latter with any degree of frequency. 71.4% consider supporting minority causes important, but only 32.8% of the priests are so occupied very frequently or frequently. 63.3% believe that teaching in Catholic schools is an important aspect of their ministry and 54.4% are so involved frequently. Bringing about social reform on the local level is rated important by 58.8% of the priests, but only

24.7% respond that this is an activity that they participate in frequently. 48.9% consider helping anti-nuclear or peace groups important, but only 19% give any time to this activity. Working with the retarded and mentally ill is important to 43.3% of the priests, with 14.6% indicating that this is something they do frequently. Bringing about better political leadership is of importance to 37.3%, and 8.8% signify that they have some involvement in this activity.

36% see providing recreational facilities for the young as an important part of their ministry, but less than half of these (15.3%) indicate that they do so frequently. 33.7% list teaching in non-Catholic schools as a ministry of some importance with only 7.6% of them so involved to any degree.

For 25.3% of the priests some association with social or civil rights groups is of some importance, but only 9.3% indicate that they are so occupied frequently. Finally, 14% see participation in some significant social action as important to their ministry, but only 3.8% actually do take part with any degree of regularity.

Analysis

I found the results of this section rather startling. For one thing, they would seem to indicate that the majority of the priests fit into the pre-Vatican Council group that I described in the first chapter of this project. I suppose that, in one sense, this really should not be so unexpected in view of the fact that the majority of the priests received their seminary training prior to the Second Vatican Council and were ordained before the close of the Council. It would appear that, although they may have moved to another position intellectually, in terms of their pastoral practice they have not moved.

The fact that there was one hundred percent agreement among the respondents about the frequency of preaching and almost as much with regard to its importance means that they see this aspect of their ministry as very essential. This is the only instance in the entire questionnaire where there was such universal agreement. That there was such high agreement and such a significant correlation between importance and frequency in the first three rankings (preaching, presiding at Eucharist, administering the Sacraments) would seem to indicate that the concentration of emphasis for most of the respondents is in areas that pertain primarily to their cultic role.

It is interesting to note that the first eleven rankings—in terms of both importance and frequency—involve the same items, though in some of them the correlation is not so great as in the first five. For example, even though the item that deals with equipping the laity to evangelize ranks sixth in importance, still, in terms of frequency, it ranks eleventh.

All the items that pertain to the social dimension of ministry have a lesser ranking than those that pertain to the work of a priest within the local parish setting, in terms of both importance and frequency. Although approximately three-quarters of the priests affirm the importance of social issues in relationship to their ministry, still the disparity between this percentage and the frequency percentage is very great. This forces one to conclude that there is not much evidence of reaching out to the larger community or of any great involvement in the social issues of the day. Even the issue of the Right to Life Movement ranks twelfth in terms of importance and fifteenth in terms of frequency. It would appear that there is a real need for a great deal of consciousness raising among the priests of the Diocese of Joliet.

Section IV—Personal Practices

Instructions: The following are some of the elements in the personal life of a priest that can be fulfilling and rewarding. For each of the items use the numbers *to signify their* importance *in your life and the* letters *signify their* frequency *in your life.*

4-Very important 3-Important 2-Somewhat important 1-Not important

A-Very frequently B-Frequently C-Infrequently D-Not at all

1. Praying to Mary.

   | (N-187) | 4 (30.5%) | 3 (36.4%) | 2 (23.5%) | 1 (9.6%) |
   | (N-186) | A (29.0%) | B (33.3%) | C (29.0%) | D (8.6%) |

2. Going to Confession.

   | (N-189) | 4 (31.2%) | 3 (46.6%) | 2 (19.6%) | 1 (2.6%) |
   | (N-186) | A (11.8%) | B (41.9%) | C (43.0%) | D (3.2%) |

3. Doing Spiritual reading.

   | (N-187) | 4 (55.0%) | 3 (37.0%) | 2 (7.4%) | 1 (0.5%) |
   | (N-187) | A (28.3%) | B (49.2%) | C (20.9%) | D (1.6%) |

4. Being with friends.

   | (N-188) | 4 (48.4%) | 3 (38.8%) | 2 (12.8%) | 1 (0.0%) |
   | (N-187) | A (27.8%) | B (50.3%) | C (20.9%) | D(1.1%) |

5. Praying the official prayer of the Church.

| (N-189) | 4 (44.4%) | 3 (33.9%) | 2 (16.4%) | 1 (5.3%) |
| (N-186) | A (48.4%) | B (31.2%) | C (16.1%) | D (4.3%) |

6. Making personal donations of money to worthy causes.

| (N-185) | 4 (27.6%) | 3 (43.2%) | 2 (22.7%) | 1 (6.5%) |
| (N-186) | A (21.2%) | B (38.6%) | C (29.9%) | D (10.3%) |

7. Taking courses/workshops in continuing education.

| (N-187) | 4 (36.4%) | 3 (41.2%) | 2 (20.3%) | 1 (2.1%) |
| (N-186) | A (13.4%) | B (40.9%) | C (37.6%) | D (8.1%) |

8. Experiencing the spiritual security that results from responding to the Divine Call.

| (N-174) | 4 (33.3%) | 3 (40.2%) | 2 (20.1%) | 1 (6.3%) |
| (N-172) | A (18.6%) | B (43.6%) | C (30.2%) | D (7.6%) |

9. Taking time off.

| (N-187) | 4 (45.5%) | 3 (39.0%) | 2 (14.4%) | 1 (1.1%) |
| (N-185) | A (14.6%) | B (39.5%) | C (42.7%) | D (3.2%) |

10. Spending time in meditation and reflection.

| (N-189) | 4 (57.7%) | 3 (36.0%) | 2 (6.3%) | 1 (0.0%) |
| (N-187) | A (27.8%) | B (47.6%) | C (23.0%) | D (1.6%) |

11. Going to plays, concerts, films, etc.

| (N-188) | 4 (11.2%) | 3 (29.8%) | 2 (43.1%) | 1 (16.0%) |
| (N-187) | A (5.3%) | B (16.6%) | C (63.6%) | D (14.4%) |

Display
Importance of Personal Practice*

Importance

Meditation.(#10)	92.7%
Doing spiritual reading. (3)	92.0%
Being with friends. (4)	87.2%
Taking time off. (9)	84.5%
Praying the Breviary. (5)	78.1%
Going to Confession. (2)	77.8%
Continuing education. (7)	77.6%
Security resulting from response to Divine Call. (8)	73.5%
Donating money. (6)	70.8%
Praying to Mary. (1)	66.9%
Going to theatre, etc. (11)	41.0%

Display
Frequency of Personal Practice**

Frequency

Praying the Breviary. (#5)	79.6%
Being with friends. (4)	78.1%
Doing spiritual reading. (3)	77.5%

*Based on responses: "Very important" and "Important."
**Based on responses: "Very frequently" and "Frequently."

Meditation. (10) 75.4%

Praying to Mary. (1) 62.3%

Security resulting from response to Divine Call. (8) 62.2%

Donating money. (6) 59.8%

Continuing education. (7) 54.3%

Taking time off. (9) 54.1%

Going to Confession. (2) 53.7%

Going to theatre, etc. (11) 21.9%

Commentary

Most of the respondents (92%) consider meditation and spiritual reading important elements in their everyday life, although the number who engage in these exercises frequently is somewhat smaller (77.5%; 75.4%). The official prayer of the Church does not rate quite so high (78.1%), nor does going to Confession (77.8%). As far as frequency is concerned, approximately an equal number (79.6%) say the Breviary frequently, but a smaller number (53.7%) approach the Sacrament of Reconciliation on a regular basis.

Being with friends is important to 87.2% of the priests, and 78.1% of them manage to do so frequently. Taking time off rates rather high (84.5%), but it is interesting to note that only 54.1% indicate that this is something they do regularly.

Slightly more than three-fourths (77.6%) see an important value in Continuing Education, but only 54.3% take advantage of it with any regularity. 73.5% experience a sense of security resulting from their response to the calling they have received, and 62.2% experience this frequently.

70.8% feel an obligation to donate money to worthy causes and 59.8% do so frequently. For slightly more than two-thirds of the priests (66.9%) Marian devotion is important, and 62.3% engage in some such devotion frequently. Finally, less than half (41%) see going to the theatre, etc. as an important element in their lives and of these slightly more than half (21.9%) do so often.

Analysis

Early on in our Doctor of Ministry Program, our co-learners were asked to do a ministry assessment analysis. The results showed, among other things, that they put a high priority on the item that referred to priests being men of prayer. In my questionnaire the fact that meditation and spiritual reading are important to so many of the priests means that priests are making a strong attempt to fulfill the laity's expectations in this regard. The fact that only slightly more than half of the respondents approach the Sacrament of Reconciliation with any degree of frequency and 21.9% do not consider it to be of importance in their lives appears to mirror the attitude of many of the laity with regard to this particular Sacrament.

84.5% of these respondents feel that taking time off is important to them, but only slightly more than half actually do so with any degree of regularity. This means that 15% do not consider it important and of those who do, 30% are not doing so. This fairly large group is exposing itself to the possibility of burn-out or some related illness. Although Bishop Imesch has emphasized to the priests their need for rest and relaxation, it would appear that the priests have not heeded his recommendation. Perhaps it is for this reason that so many find themselves in stressful situations, an area that we will consider next.

Section V—Sources of Stress

In the previous two sections I combined the percentages for the "very important" and "important" categories because I believe the division between these and the "somewhat important" and "not important" categories is rather marked. I did the same thing for this section and found that the percentages of responses were somewhat lower than in Section III and Section IV. Since this topic of stress is a very important one, I thought it best to include the "very stressful," "stressful," and "somewhat stressful" responses under one percentage category to allow for the various nuances implied. I include a display for both approaches with regard to degree. Please note that although the percentages in the second display are higher, with either arrangement the same sources of stress, for the most part, can be found at the top, in the middle or toward the bottom of the ratings.

Sources of Stress

Instructions: The following are some of the situations in the life of a priest that can cause stress. For each of the items use the numbers *to signify the* degree of stress *in your life and the* letters *to indicate* frequency of stress.

4-Very stressful 3-Stressful 2-Somewhat stressful 1-Not stressful at all

A-Very frequently B-Frequently C-Infrequently D-Not at all

1. The amount of administrative work I have to do.

   (N-184)   4 (10.3%)   3 (31.5%)   2 (44.0%)   1 (14.1%)
   (N-183)   A (18.6%)   B (34.4%)   C (36.6%)   D (10.4%)

2. The maintenance of morale among staff members.

   (N-177)   4 (15.8%)   3 (31.6%)   2 (31.1%)   1 (21.5%)
   (N-177)   A (13.6%)   B (32.8%)   C (41.8%)   D (11.9%)

3. The apathy and indifference among laity.

   (N-183)   4 (12.0%)   3 (27.9%)   2 (45.4%)   1 (14.8%)
   (N-179)   A (7.8%)   B (31.8%)   C (49.7%)   D (10.6%)

4. The vocal minority who are hypercritical.

   (N-182)   4 (17.6%)   3 (26.9%)   2 (36.3%)   1 (19.2%)
   (N-180)   A (3.3%)   B (21.1%)   C (54.4%)   D (21.1%)

5. Behind-the-back criticism.

   (N-181)   4 (18.2%)   3 (28.7%)   2 (32.6%)   1 (20.4%)
   (N-178)   A (2.8%)   B (16.9%)   C (60.7%)   D (19.7%)

6. The number of meetings that I am required to attend.

   (N-182)   4 (20.3%)   3 (30.2%)   2 (37.9%)   1 (11.5%)
   (N-179)   A (19.6%)   B (37.4%)   C (33.5%)   D (9.5%)

7. The lack of support and recognition from my Ordinary.

   (N-182)   4 (14.8%)   3 (13.7%)   2 (23.1%)   1 (48.4%)
   (N-182)   A (11.0%)   B 11.0%)   C (27.5%)   D (50.5%)

8. The lack of support and recognition from my fellow priests.

| (N-183) | 4 (10.4%) | 3 (24.6%) | 2 (29.0) | 1 (36.1%) |
| (N-181) | A (8.8%) | B (18.2%) | C (36.5%) | D (36.5%) |

9. The lack of visible results from my ministry.

| (N-184) | 4 (6.0%) | 3 (18.5%) | 2 (47.8%) | 1 (27.7%) |
| (N-182) | A (3.3%) | B (17.6%) | C (54.4%) | D (24.7%) |

10. The dichotomy that exists between magisterial statements and the beliefs and practices of many Catholics.

| (N-181) | 4 (11.6%) | 3 (34.8%) | 2 (38.1%) | 1 (15.5%) |
| (N-178) | A (15.2%) | B (30.9%) | C (37.6%) | D (16.3%) |

11. Inability to talk about my spiritual values and prayer life.

| (N-183) | 4 (3.8%) | 3 (7.3%) | 2 (40.4%) | 1 (46.4%) |
| (N-178) | A (2.2%) | B (12.4%) | C (40.5%) | D (44.9%) |

12. Sense of estrangement from my peers.

| (N-185) | 4 (5.9%) | 3 (14.6%) | 2 (29.2%) | 1 (50.3%) |
| (N-181) | A (4.4%) | B (14.8%) | C (31.7%) | D (49.2%) |

13. Sharing ministry with laity, especially women.

| (N-184) | 4 (1.6%) | 3 (3.8%) | 2 (29.3%) | 1 (65.2%) |
| (N-182) | A (6.0%) | B (5.5%) | C (31.3%) | D (57.1%) |

14. Lack of support and recognition from the laity.

| (N-184) | 4 (1.1%) | 3 (13.0%) | 2 (42.9%) | 1 (42.9%) |
| (N-181) | A (2.8%) | B (8.8%) | C (44.8%) | D (43.6%) |

15. Coping with the sense of loneliness.

| (N-182) | 4 (10.4%) | 3 (26.9%) | 2 (45.1) | 1 (17.6%) |
| (N-176) | A (5.1%) | B (23.3%) | C (55.1%) | D (16.5%) |

16. Dealing with routineness resulting from frequent celebration of Eucharist.

| (N-183) | 4 (2.2%) | 3 (12.6%) | 2 (43.7%) | 1 (41.5%) |
| (N-179) | A (2.2%) | B (10.6%) | C (46.9%) | D (40.2%) |

17. Developing and maintaining healthy relationships with women.

| (N-183) | 4 (1.6%) | 3 (8.2%) | 2 (38.3%) | 1 (51.9%) |
| (N-179) | A (2.2%) | B (11.2%) | C (41.9%) | D (44.7%) |

18. Dealing with the spiritual needs of others on a one-to-one basis.

| (N-183) | 4 (1.6%) | 3 (15.8%) | 2 (39.9%) | 1 (42.6%) |
| (N-179) | A (7.3%) | B (22.3%) | C (39.7%) | D (30.7%) |

19. Coping with aridity in my spiritual life.

| (N-182) | 4 (2.7%) | 3 (29.7%) | 2 (46.7%) | 1 (20.9%) |
| (N-176) | A (1.7%) | B (26.7%) | C (52.8%) | D (18.8%) |

20. Handling the demands made on my time and talents.

| (N-184) | 4 (21.7%) | 3 (34.8%) | 2 (27.7%) | 1 (15.8%) |
| (N-180) | A (16.7%) | B (42.8%) | C (26.7%) | D (13.9%) |

21. Struggling to be faithful to my celibate commitment.

| (N-184) | 4 (10.9%) | 3 (23.9%) | 2 (41.3%) | 1 (23.9%) |
| (N-179) | A (6.7%) | B (27.9%) | C (42.5%) | D (22.9%) |

22. Feeling dependent on the institutional Church.

| (N-184) | 4 (3.8%) | 3 (8.7%) | 2 (34.2%) | 1 (53.3%) |
| (N-179) | A (3.4%) | B (10.1%) | C (34.1%) | D (52.5%) |

23. Dealing with different conflicts connected with rectory living.

| (N-177) | 4 (10.2%) | 3 (22.6%) | 2 (33.3%) | 1 (33.9%) |
| (N-171) | A (7.6%) | B (18.1%) | C (39.8%) | D (34.5%) |

Display
Relative Degrees of Sources of Stress*

Demands on time and talent. (#20) 56.5%

Required meetings. (6) 50.5%

Morale maintenance. (2) 47.4%

Behind-the-back criticism. (5) 46.9%

Dichotomy between teaching and practice. (10) . . 46.4%

Hypercritical vocal minority. (4) 44.5%

Administrative work required. (1) 41.8%

Lay apathy and indifference. (3) 39.9%

Coping with loneliness. (15) 37.3%

Lack of peer support and recognition. (8) . . . 35.0%

Struggle with celibacy. (21) 34.8%

Conflicts in rectory living. (23) 32.8%

Coping with aridity. (19) 32.4%

*Responses ranked according to categories of "Very stressful," and "Stressful."

Lack of support from ordinary. (7) 28.5%

Lack of visible results. (9) 24.5%

Peer estrangement. (12) 20.5%

Dealing with others' spiritual needs. (18) 17.4%

Routineness of Eucharist. (16) 14.8%

Lack of lay support and recognition. (14) 14.1%

Inability to talk about own spiritual values. (11) . . 13.1%

Healthy female relationships. (17) 12.5%

Dependency on institutional church. (22) 9.8%

Sharing ministry with laity, especially women. (13) . 5.4%

Display
Relative Degrees of Sources of Stress*

Required meetings. (#6) 88.5%

Administrative work required. (1) 85.9%

Lay apathy and indifference. (3) 85.2%

Dichotomy between teaching and practice. (10) . . 84.5%

Demands on time and talent. (20) 84.2%

Coping with loneliness. (15) 82.4%

Hypercritical vocal minority. (4) 80.8%

Behind-the-back criticism. (5) 79.6%

Coping with aridity. (19) 79.1%

*Responses ranked according to categories of "Very stressful," "Stressful," and "Some-what stressful."

Morale maintenance. (2) 78.5%

Struggle with celibacy. (21) 76.1%

Lack of visible results. (9) 72.3%

Conflicts in rectory living. (23) 66.1%

Lack of peer support and recognition. (8) 63.9%

Routineness of Eucharist. (16) 58.5%

Dealing with others' spiritual needs. (18) 57.4%

Lack of lay support and recognition. (14) 57.1%

Peer estrangement. (12) 49.7%

Healthy female relationships. (17) 48.1%

Dependency on institutional church. (22) 46.7%

Inability to talk about own spiritual values. (11) . . 43.6%

Lack of support from Ordinary. (7) 41.6%

Sharing ministry with laity, especially women. (13) 34.8%

Display
Frequency of Sources of Stress*

Handling demands on time and talent. (#20) . . . 59.9%

Number of meetings to attend. (6) 57.0%

Administrative work. (1) 53.0%

Morale maintenance. (2) 46.4%

Dichotomy between teaching and practice. (10) . . 46.1%

*Responses ranked according to categories "Very frequently" and "Frequently."

Lay apathy and indifference. (3) 39.6%

Struggle with celibacy. (21) 34.6%

Dealing with others' spiritual needs. (18) 29.6%

Coping with aridity. (19) 28.4%

Coping with loneliness. (15) 28.4%

Lack of peer support. (8) 27.0%

Conflicts in rectory living. (23) 25.7%

Hypercritical vocal minority. (4) 24.4%

Lack of support from Ordinary. (7) 22.0%

Lack of visible results. (9) 20.9%

Behind-the-back criticism. (5) 19.7%

Peer estrangement. (12) 19.2%

Inability to talk about spiritual values. (11) . . . 14.6%

Dependency on institutional church. (22) 13.5%

Healthy female relationships. (17) 13.4%

Routine celebration of Eucharist. (16) 12.8%

Lack of lay support and recognition. (14) 11.6%

Sharing ministry with laity, especially women. (13) . 11.5%

Commentary

88.5% of the priests consider the meetings they are required to attend a source of stress, and 57% report that they feel stress very frequently or at least frequently. Administrative work bothers 85.9% of the respondents, with 53% of them indicating that they are so bothered with some degree of frequency. 85.2% feel some tension because of the apathy and indifference they perceive among the laity, but only 39.6% experience this stress with any regularity.

84.5% have some difficulty handling the dichotomy that exists between magisterial statements and the beliefs and practices of many Catholics, and for approximately half (46.4%), this occurs frequently. The demands made on their time and talents is a source of stress for 84.2% of the priests with this item having the highest percentage of frequency—59.9%

Coping with a sense of loneliness is a problem for 82.4% of the respondents, but only 28.4% signified that this gets to them frequently. 80.8% have trouble dealing with the vocal minority who are hypercritical, with 24.4% indicating some degree of frequency.

Behind-the-back criticism takes its toll on 79.6% of the priests and 19.7% feel the stress frequently. 79.1% report that they have difficulty coping with aridity in their own spiritual lives, but it is a regular experience for only 28.4% of the priests. For 78.5%, maintaining morale among staff members causes stress and more than half consider it something they deal with frequently.

76.1% consider their struggle with celibacy a stressful situation and for 34.6% it occurs with some frequency. Lack of visible results in their ministry causes 72.3% some anxiety, with 20.9% reporting that it is frequently a problem for them. For 66.1% of the priests the conflicts they experience living in a rectory causes tension in their lives, but only 25.7% experience this stress with any regularity.

Lack of support from their fellow priests is a source of stress for 63.9% of the priests, and 27% feel the stress frequently. 58.5%

have some difficulty handling the routineness resulting from the regular celebration of the Eucharist, but only 12.8% cite this as something that occurs frequently. Dealing with the spiritual needs of others causes some anxious moments for 57.4%, and for 29.6% the moments happen with some degree of frequency.

57.1% are bothered by the lack of support and recognition on the part of the laity, but only 11.6% signify that they are so bothered frequently. Estrangement from their fellow clergy causes some trouble for 49.7% of the priests, with 19.2% indicating that the problem crops up regularly.

Developing and maintaining healthy relationships with women causes stress for almost half of the respondents (48.1%), but it would appear to be something that occurs frequently for only 13.4% of the priests polled. 46.7% checked the item dealing with dependency on the institutional church as a source of stress, but again only a small percentage (13.5%) cited it as something that they had to contend with frequently. A certain inability to talk about their own spiritual life and values causes 43.6% of the priests some stress, with 14.6% indicating that it is a problem they face frequently. Lack of support and recognition from the Ordinary is stressful to some degree for 41.6% of the priests, and for 22% of them it is a source of tension that they have to deal with frequently. Finally, both in terms of degree and frequency, sharing ministry with the laity, especially women, was the item least cited—34.8% with regard to degree and 11.5% with regard to frequency.

In this section I provided space for the respondents to add any sources of stress they experienced that had not been mentioned already. Thirty-eight of the priests opted to do so and listed a total of sixty-two items. There was no one major theme running through these responses. Coping with disobedience to the magisterium was cited in some form five times and pastor-associate conflicts four times. For the most part, however, the sources of stress that were added were very disparate.

Analysis

I consider it quite an alarming fact that more than fifty percent of the respondents see the majority of the items in this section of the questionnaire to be stressful to some degree, even though the percentages of those who found them occurring in their lives very frequently are not so high. No one expects the life of a priest to be stressless or even any less stressful than the life of any human being. However, the fact that so many of the priests responded the way they did in this section suggests that a program or workshop dealing with ways of coping with stress would be very much in order. At the very least, the priests should be greatly and frequently encouraged to seek out a counselor to assist them in coping with the various sources of stress in their everyday lives. Problems in the area of physical health and departures from the active ministry would perhaps be greatly reduced.

Section VI—Free Association

Instructions: On the line opposite each of the following words or expressions write the first word or expression that comes to your mind.

1. GOD _____
2. JESUS CHRIST _____
3. BIBLE _____
4. GRACE _____
5. CHURCH _____
6. ECCLESIAL _____

I included this section in the questionnaire mainly to see if there would be any unusual or significant responses. The results, however, revealed nothing really startling. In the event that the reader may wish to have some idea as to what the responses were, give a summary of the major reactions to the six terms cited.

GOD		JESUS CHRIST	
Loving Father	- 71	Hope/Savior	- 57
Love	- 16	Brother	- 28
Creator	- 8	Friend	- 20
All Powerful	- 7	Lord	- 16
Good	- 6	Love	- 14
Life	- 6	Redeemer	- 10
Christ	- 6	Son	- 8
Supreme Ruler	- 3	Example/Model	- 5
Mystery	- 3	Kindness	- 5
		God/Man	- 4

BIBLE		GRACE	
God's Word	- 70	Life	- 39
The Good Book	- 8	Free Gift of God	- 19
Inspirational	- 8	Help	- 16
Faith Story	- 7	Love	- 12
Good News	- 6	Presence	- 10
Word of Life	- 6	God's Love	- 9
Bread of Life	- 5	Absolutely Necessary	- 9
		Strength	- 8
		Power	- 6
		Happiness	- 4

CHURCH		ECCLESIAL AUTHORITY	
People	- 45	Bishop	- 20
Community	- 26	Necessary	- 17
Family	- 14	Power	- 9
Mother	- 11	God's Guiding Hand	- 8
Body of Christ	- 10	Pope	- 7
Institution	- 9	Hierarchy	- 7
Home	- 5	Leaders	- 7
		Legalism	- 6

In the final category, five chose such expressions as "Obedience," "Weak," "Frustration," "Helpful and supportive." Three wrote words such as "Us" (sic), "Rigid" and "Problematic."

To each of the six words the rest of the priests responded with a variety of different, individual expressions.

Section VII—Motivations For Remaining Active

Instructions: The following are some motivating factors that may contribute to your decision to remain active in priestly ministry. please circle the number on each line that best reflects your attitude toward each statement in terms of your own life.

4-Very Important 3-Important 2-Somewhat Important 1-Not Important

1. I feel that I am making a real contribution to the mission of the Church. (N-183)

    4 (55.2%)   3 (36.6%)   2 (8.2%)   1 (0.0%)

2. I experience a great deal of satisfaction in the work I do. (N-184)

   4 (46.7%)   3 (40.8%)   2 (12.0%)   1 (0.5%)

3. I am able to have an impact on the lives of individuals in a very special way. (N-184)

   4 (50.5%)   3 (39.7%)   2 (9.2%)   1 (0.5%)

4. I believe that the priesthood provides me with the best opportunity to save my soul. (N-186)

   4 (32.6%)   3 (25.5%)   2 (23.9%)   1 (17.9%)

5. I experience a sense of purposefulness as a result of my response to God's call. (N-186)

   4 (45.2%)   3 (44.6%)   2 (9.7%)   1 (0.5%)

6. I experience a sense of excitement in meeting the challenges associated with priesthood today. (N-184)

   4 (34.2%)   3 (36.4%)   2 (26.6%)   1 (2.7%)

7. I enjoy the power and influence within the Church and society that flow from priesthood. (N-184)

   4 (6.0%)   3 (17.9%)   2 (34.8%)   1 (41.3%)

8. I like the creature comforts and the fringe benefits the priesthood provides. (N-182)

   4 (1.6%)   3 (8.2%)   2 (38.5%)   1 (51.6%)

9. I have been a priest for too many years to consider any other way of life. (N-183)

4 (14.2%)   3 (16.4%)   2 (15.8%)   1 (53.6%)

10. I experience a great deal of satisfaction knowing that I have been and continue to be faithful to my priestly commitment. (N-184)

4 (34.8%)   3 (37.5%)   2 (2.1.7%)   1 (6.0%)

11. I like the fact that I am able to be a force for good in the struggle to realize the Kingdom of God here on earth. (N-185)

4 (47.0%)   3 (35.7%)   2 (17.3%)   1 (0.0%)

12. I believe that the people see me as a special sign of God's presence in the world. (N-183)

4 (30.1%)   3 (45.4%)   2 (20.2%)   1 (4.4%)

13. I do not wish to experience the uncertainty that would be associated with a vocational change. (N-183)

4 (15.3%)   3 (13.1%)   2 (25.7%)   1 (45.9%)

Display
Motivations For Remaining Active

I feel that I am making a real contribution
to the mission of the Church. (#1) 91.8%

I am able to have an impact on the lives
of individuals in a very special way. (3)   .   .   . 90.2%

I experience a sense of purposefulness
as a result of my response to God's call. (5)   .   . 89.8%

I experience a great deal of satisfaction
in the work I do. (2) 87.5%

I like the fact that I am able to be a
force for good in the struggle to realize
the Kingdom of God here on earth. (11)   .   .   . 82.7%

I believe that the people see me as a
special sign of God's presence in the
world. (12) 75.5%

I experience a great deal of satisfaction
knowing that I have been and continue to be
faithful to my priestly commitment. (10)   .   .   . 72.3%

I experience a sense of excitement in
meeting the challenges associated with
priesthood today. (6) 70.6%

I believe that the priesthood provides
me with the best opportunity to save my
soul. (4) 58.1%

I have been a priest for too many years
to consider any other way of life. (9) 30.6%

I do not wish to experience the uncertainty
that would be associated with a vocational
change. (13) 28.4%

I enjoy the power and influence within
the Church and society that flow from
priesthood. (7) 23.9%

I like the creature comforts and the
fringe benefits the priesthood provides. (8)   .   . 9.8%

Commentary

91.8% of the respondents feel that the idea they are making a real contribution to the mission of the Church is a very important or important reason for their remaining active in ministry. 90.2% cited the fact that they are able to have an impact on the lives of individuals as an important motive. A sense of purposefulness as a result of their response to God's call was considered to be important by 89.9% of the priests. The satisfaction they experience in the work they do is a reason for 87.5%, and being a force for good in the struggle to realize the Kingdom of God here on earth motivates 82.7%.

74.5% of the priests believe that people see them as special signs of God's presence in the world and so they consider this to be an important factor in their decision to remain active. The satisfaction they derive from knowing that they are faithful to their priestly commitment is an important reason for 72.3%. The excitement associated with meeting the challenges involved in priesthood today influences 70.6%.

58.1% see the fact that the priesthood provides them with the best opportunity to save their souls as a very important or at least important reason. 30.6% indicated that, having been in the priesthood for so many years, they do not wish to consider another way of life.

28.4% admitted that not wanting to experience the uncertainty associated with a vocation change affects their choice. The power and influence within the Church and society that flow from priesthood was cited by 23.9% of the priests. Finally, only 9.4% see the creature comforts and fringe benefits the priesthood provides as a factor in their decision to remain active.

Again the respondents were offered the opportunity to mention other factors they considered of some import, but only twenty-four opted to do so. The reasons they advanced were basically restatements of the items dealing with the topics of satisfaction and their response to God's call.

Analysis

Contributing to the mission of the Church and being a force for good in the struggle to realize the Kingdom of God here on earth are reasons cited by a goodly number of the priests. This means that they see themselves as being actively involved in an operation of immense scope affecting not just their immediate locale, but the whole world. Because of this, their lives take on added meaning.

The impact they have on others, the knowledge that they are responding to God's call and the satisfaction they experience from the work they do were factors that a significant number of the priests checked. This indicates that they realize a great deal of self-fulfillment in their ministry and so do not face any degree of dissatisfaction that would prompt them to look elsewhere.

The sense of excitement they feel in meeting the challenges associated with the priesthood was also rated important by many of the priests. This means that they do not find their way of life boring. Fidelity to their priestly commitment and their belief that people perceive them as special signs of God's presence in the world are also important for many of them. This would lead one to conclude that their self-image is greatly enhanced because they are seen as faithful, responsible people who have a special relationship with the Lord. This also indicates that they appreciate the symbolic value of their priesthood.

Power and influence as well as creature comforts and fringe benefits were rated as very important or important by the least number of respondents. The fact that power and influence were rated by such a small percentage is in sharp contrast to the percentage who indicated that having an impact on people's lives and being a force for good were very important or important. This would seem to mean that a goodly number are not willing to admit that the element of power has a great deal to do with the helping professions, of which the priesthood is certainly one. At the very least, one would have to say that many do not seem to be even aware that there is a relationship between power and priesthood.

Section VIII—Vocation Recruitment

Instructions: In column "A," circle the code following the statement which most accurately reflects your attitude toward recruiting for the priesthood at the present time. *In column "B," circle the code following the statement which most accurately reflects your attitude toward recruiting for the priesthood* five years ago.

1. I actively encourage men to enter the seminary.

(N-139)* A (36.0%)   (N-129)** B (44.2%)

2. I encourage men but advise them about the uncertainties and tensions that surround the role of the priest today.

A (38.1%)   B (24.0%)

3. I neither encourage nor discourage men, but allow them to make up their own minds.

A (21.6%)   B (26.4%)

*Number who responded regarding attitudes "at present time."
**Number who responded regarding attitudes "five years ago."

4. I tend to discourage men from entering now and advise them to wait until the future is more certain.

A (2.2%)   B (3.9%)

5. Other (Please describe)_____

_____

A (2.2%)   B (1.6%)

The first thing I would ask the reader to note is the fact that the percentage of priests responding to this section was quite low. Some of the respondents indicated that they were unable to make sense out of the directions, while others failed to circle anything. However, those who pre-tested the questionnaire had no difficulty with this section. Perhaps the priests were exhausted by the time they came to this topic!!!

36% of those who did respond indicated that, at the time the questionnaire was administered, they actively encouraged men to enter the seminary, whereas 44.2% acknowledged that they had done so five years previously. 38.1% encouraged but advised men about the uncertainties and tensions, but previously 24% used this approach. 21.6% neither encouraged nor discouraged people from entering, while five years before, 26.4% felt this to be the best way to handle the situation. 2.2% tended to discourage men from entering and advised them to wait, with 3.9% adopting this attitude five years previously.

These results mean that in 1984 fewer priests were actively seeking recruits than five years prior to that time. A higher percentage were encouraging but putting more limitations on their enthusiasm than in 1979. Although a smaller percentage was adopting a "hands off" attitude as compared with the way some of the priests operated five years before, and a smaller percentage discouraged men than did in 1979, still these latter percentages in these categories are significant. All the figures for 1984 would seem to indicate that the fervor of priests in this area leaves something to be desired. Perhaps this report will spark further activity on the part of the diocesan administration as well as on the part of priests themselves.

Section IX—Varia

A. Of the following four categories, _____best describes my outlook on life and priesthood at the present time. (N-183)

1) Very Satisfied   (37.2%)
2) Quite Satisfied   (50.3%)
3) Not Too Satisfied   (12.0%)
4) Very Unsatisfied   (0.5%)

I believe these percentages speak for themselves. The fact that 87.5% of the priests acknowledge that they are satisfied (very or quite) suggests a positive outlook on their life and ministry. I found a correlation here with the response to the second statement in Section VII. There, 46.7% responded that they considered satisfaction in the work they do an important reason for remaining active in ministry; 40.8% felt it important; 12% somewhat important and .5% not important. The first two percentages add up to 87.5% and the latter two are the same in both Section VII and Section IX.

B. On the back of this sheet of paper, please describe what you consider to be your role in priestly ministry today.

The invitation to put down what they considered the role of the priest to be in ministry today was ignored by sixty of the respondents. Thirty-eight wrote a sentence or phrase and eighty-eight took the time to write a paragraph, essay or outline. I shall conclude this section with a representative sampling of their comments. Which paragraphs and essays to select proved to be rather difficult because so many of them were truly interesting.

- A proclaimer of the Good News of the Lord

- To preach the Good News by Word and Example.

- An enabler.

- To be an instrument of Christ for others.

- To companion others on their walk through life.

- Serve people.

- To be minister of the word and sacrament.

- To do God's will (in my regard) as I see and understand it.

- To empower the laity to take responsibility for the mission of the Church in the areas of service to others, worship and education.

- To pray, to proclaim, to preside, to share my faith, to counsel, to console, to be present to.

* * * * * * * * * *

- Good preaching and very visible presence as a loving and faithful disciple are important aspects of the role for me now. I also think it is important for the priest to challenge the community to move toward evangelization and ecumenism.

- As priest, I see my "work" to be the coordinator of many ministries, to be a leader, support and "trainer" (or provide this service) for God's people so that Jesus' Good News and Mission to build the Kingdom may be continued and proclaimed.

- I believe in all the traditional priestly activities which include administration of the sacraments, giving guidance on the way to salvation and holiness, leading in prayer, coordinating various parish activities, etc.

* * * * * * * * *

I consider my role as:

1. Proclaimer of the Word.

   If God spoke to His people, then the Word must be proclaimed so people can hear it. But I must first live that Word—embody the Word to shape my life.

2. Presider at Sacraments.

   I must lead the people in prayer as a response to the Word. I must first be a person in prayer.

3. Pastor or leader.

   I must create a condition for the community to function—enabling the people to use their gifts for the benefit of all. I must accept responsibility, however, to lead and use my gifts to influence change in the community.

* * * * * * * * *

I am not "discouraged" with the lack of priests. The laity is being called to fulfill its ministerial role in the Church. Today, we, as priests, must be "enablers"—giving the people of God what is theirs by virtue of their baptism. As priests we, in a sense, must decrease.

The Church of Tomorrow is a Church not of "priests" but of the laity. I feel joyous in this thought. Our present poverty is, in reality, our strength, if we but have eyes to see. As pastor of a rather large parish, I say quite emphatically, "They, the laity, must increase, and we must decrease. I realize, of course, that few 'priests-bishops' would agree."

* * * * * * * * * *

My priestly role in the ministry today is no different than it was over twenty years ago when I was ordained . . . it is clearly defined in the instruction given by the bishop at the time of ordination. Essentially to offer the Sacrifice of the Mass, administer the Sacraments and Preach the word of God in my daily life. Anything beyond that you need not be ordained to do.

* * * * * * * * * *

My role in priestly ministry today is to try with all the talents God has given to make the Paschal Mystery come alive in God's People; to help people be caught up in that process, to experience the power of God in their lives; to help them come alive in every way, given that the "Glory of God is in man fully alive." To Him be all the Glory and Honor—in and through Jesus Christ, by the power of the Holy Spirit—even as I am caught up in it with them.

* * * * * * * * * *

As an ordained priest, I perceive my role first to hear the Word in Scripture; my life; my environment; to reflect on the Word; and to preach the Word from the vantage of my witness.

Second. To preside at the liturgical actions of the faith community.

Third. To organize the life of the community by discerning the giftedness of individuals and empowering them by affirmation to exercise their gifts on behalf of the community, church and/or world.

* * * * * * * * * *

A leader who does not give up or forfeit his duty and right to lead—a duty and right that have their roots in his ministerial priesthood—both in the celebration of the liturgy and in the running of parish life as a whole.

A facilitator: a man who helps people to be more; better Christians; a man who helps Catholics to witness to each other and to those who are not Catholic by what they say and do.

* * * * * * * * * *

To be a servant of Our Lord in the Church as a shepherd; proclaiming the teaching in the Gospel, administering the sacraments, guiding the faithful in their efforts to form Christian ideals, and then in the struggle to realize them, being an animator of the faithful in their apostolate of building God's Kingdom in the secular world.

* * * * * * * * * *

My role in priesthood today is to try to be a bridge between what priesthood has been before Vatican II and during the ensuing twenty years into the new, changed priesthood evolving out of a new Kairos. It is a time of passage, as was described at a Vatican meeting in December,1983. How can we help the transition from a clerical church to a lay church and, in the process, make greater gains with a diminishing of losses. But as this process goes on, to really deepen the spirituality of myself and the people I work with through a balanced blending of the Bread of Life in both Word and Sacrament. My own personhood is the tool the Lord wants to use, my person spiritualized.

Conclusion

Three years ago, when I composed the first chapter of this project, I stated toward the end that "there will always be at least three different groups of priests—those who hold to the traditional approach to priesthood, for whom the transcendence of God and the Divinity of Christ will be of utmost importance, and whose priesthood will reflect this; those who put more stress on God's immanence and on Jesus' humanity and who will try to discern the 'signs of the time' and remain open to new possibilities; and, finally, those who will be somewhere in the middle." I believe that responses to the questionnaire prove the truth of this statement. If one looks beyond the responses themselves, one can see indications of these three perspectives.

If one examines the results of the questionnaire closely, I believe that s/he cannot possibly help but come to the following or similar conclusions. First of all, it should be quite obvious that there is a vocation crisis in the Diocese of Joliet, given the high median age of the priests and the paucity of vocations at the present time. Despite this fact, it is interesting to note that special ministries are given more attention today than in times past. The lack of minority representation among the clergy in a diocese where there is a significant Hispanic minority is an issue that cannot be swept under the table.

It seems quite evident that celibacy is not a burning issue among the priests associated with the Diocese of Joliet. There is general acceptance of laity and women being involved in ministry within the

Church, but it does not seem to be very clear that a majority work strenuously to bring this about. There does not appear to be too much familiarity with current literature concerning the theology of priesthood, nor is there much interest or involvement in social justice issues on the part of many.

Meditation and spiritual reading serve as the bulwark for the priests' spirituality and it is perhaps these that enable the priests to cope with a variety of sources of stress that plague them. A high degree of idealism and a real sense of being of service to others motivate them in their decision to remain active in priestly ministry. Finally, although the priests for the most part indicated that they were very satisfied or quite satisfied with their vocational choice, they are not overly enthusiastic about recruiting young men to follow in their footsteps.

I am not so naive as to think that this project will attract worldwide attention, but I do believe that it still has some relative importance at least for me and those who are involved in the Diocese of Joliet. One of the significant aspects of this project is the number of priests who took time to fill out and return the questionnaire. I cannot believe that anyone was in any way coerced to respond simply because Bishop Imesch wrote a cover letter. I feel certain that I was not the cause, since I was neither well-known nor a popular figure in the diocese. Perhaps a clue can be found in the alacrity with which the priests did respond. The fact that almost two hundred questionnaires were returned within two weeks would seem to indicate that the priests saw this as an opportunity to express their thoughts on matters of great import to them. As several of the priests indicated, the questionnaire provided them with an opportunity to reflect on various aspects of their priesthood. For myself, the project has clarified my understanding of and deepened my appreciation for priesthood and fills me with hope for the future, despite storm clouds on the horizon.

There may be other dioceses interested in undertaking a similar study of their priests, utilizing the questionnaire that has been developed here. I plan to offer the results to the Personnel Board of the Diocese of Joliet and to the Bishops' Committee on Priestly Formation. Perhaps one day this project will be of interest to a much wider audience than was originally envisioned.

Bibliography

Books

As One Who Serves: Reflections on the Pastoral Ministry in the United States. Prepared for the Bishops' Committee on Priestly Life and Ministry. Washington, USCC, 1977.

Baum, Gregory. *Man Becoming.* New York: Herder & Herder, 1970.

Bausch William. *Traditions, Tensions, Transitions in Ministry.* Mystic, CT: Twenty-Third Publications, 1982.

Braxton, Edward. *The Wisdom Community.* New York/Ramsey: Paulist Press, 1980.

Brown, Raymond. *The Churches the Apostles Left Behind.* New York/Ramsey: Paulist Press, 1984.

_____, et al. *Priest and Bishop: Biblical Reflections.* New York: Paulist Press, 1970.

Bunnik, Rudd. *Priests for Tomorrow.* New York: Holt, Rinehart and Winston, 1969.

Chicago Studies 20 (Spring 1981). Six essays on Sexuality and the Priesthood.

Curran, Charles E. *The Crisis in Priestly Ministry.* Notre Dame, Indiana: Fides Publishers, Inc., 1972.

Edwards, Paul. *The Theology of the Priesthood*. Hales Corners, WI., 1974.

Ernst, Cornelius. *The Theology of Grace*. Notre Dame, Indiana: Fides Publishers, Inc., 1974.

Essays on the Priesthood. St. Meinrad, Indiana: St. Meinrad's Press, 1954.

Gibbons, James Cardinal. *The Ambassador of Christ*. Baltimore, 1896.

Greeley, Andrew. *The American Catholic: A Social Portrait*. News York: Basic Books, Inc., 1977.

_____, et al. *The New Agenda*. Garden City, New York: Doubleday & Company, 1973.

_____, et al. *Parish, Priest and People*. Chicago: Thomas More Press, 1981.

Grollenberg, Lucas et al. *Minister, Pastor, Prophet*. New York: Crossroads, 1981.

Haight, S.J., Roger. *The Experience and Language of Grace*. New York/Ramsey/Toronto: Paulist Press, 1979.

Hurley, Denis and Cunnane, Joseph. *Vatican II on Priests and Seminaries*. Dublin/Chicago: Scepter, 1967.

Kasper, Walter. *An Introduction to Christian Faith*. New York/Ramsey: Paulist Press, 1980.

Kennedy, Eugene F. and Heckler, Victor J. *The Catholic Priest in the United States: Psychological Investigations*. Washington: USCC, 1972.

Kung, Hans. *On Being a Christian.* Garden City, New York: Doubleday & Company, 1976.

Lane, Dermot. *The Experience of God.* New York/Ramsey: Paulist Press, 1981.

Larkin, Ernest and Broccolo, Gerard. *Spiritual Renewal of the American Priesthood.* Washington: USCC, 1973.

Lonergan, Bernard. *Collection.* New York: Herder & Herder, 1967.

Mitchell, Nathan. *Mission and Ministry: History and Theology in the Sacrament of Order.* Wilmington, Delaware: Micheal Glazier, 1982.

Mohler, James. *The Origin and Evolution of the Priesthood.* New York: Alba House, 1970.

National Opinion Research Center. *The Catholic Priest in the United States: Sociological Investigations.* Washington: USCC, 1972.

O'Meara, Thomas. *Theology of Ministry.* New York/Ramsey: Paulist Press, 1983.

Power, David. *Gifts That Differ: Lay Ministries Established and Unestablished.* New York: Pueblo Press, 1980.

The Pope Speaks. Washington: USCC, 1973.

The Priest and Stress. Washington: USCC, 1982.

Rahner, Karl. *The Priesthood.* New York: The Seabury Press, 1973.

_____, "The Abiding Significance of the Second Vatican Council." *Theological Investigations* 20: 90-102. Translated by Edward Quinn. London: Darton, Longman and Todd, 1981.

_____, "How the Priest Should View His Official Ministry." *Theological Investigations* 14: 202-219. Translated by David Bourke. London: Darton, Longman and Todd, 1976.

_____, "The New Image of the Church." *Theological Investigations* 10:3-29. Translated by David Bourke. London: Darton, Longman and Todd, 1973.

_____, "Theological Reflections on the Priestly Image of Today and Tomorrow." *Theological Investigations* 12:39-60. Translated by David Bourke. London: Darton, Longman and Todd, 1974.

_____, ed., *Concilium 43 Identity of the Priest*. New York: Paulist Press, 1969.

Sanks, T. Howland. *Authority in the Church—A Study in Changing Paradigms*. (Dissertation Series 2, American Academy of Religion and Scholars' Press), University of Montana Printing Department, Missoula, Montana, 1974.

Schillebeeckx, Edward. *Ministry*. New York: Crossroads, 1981.

Schuller, David, Strommen, Merton and Brekke, Milo, eds. *Ministry in America*. New York: Harper & Row, 1980.

III Synod of Bishops. *The Ministerial Priesthood and Justice in the World*. Washington, USCC, 1972.

Vogels, Hans-Jurgen. "The Community's Right to a Priest in Collision with Compulsory Celibacy." In *Concilium 133 Right of the Community to a Priest,* pp. 84-92. Edited by Edward Schillebeeckx and J. Metz. New York: Seabury Press, 1980.

Whitehead, Evelyn, ed. *The Parish in Commuity and Ministry.* New York: Paulist Press, 1978.

Articles

Brown, Raymond. "The Challenge of the Three Biblical Priesthoods." *St. Mary's Seminary and University Bulletin.* (Autumn 1979): 23-27.

Coleman, John. "The Future of Ministry." *America* (March 28, 1981): 243-249.

Fink, Peter. "The Other Side of Priesthood." *America* (April 11, 1981): 291-294.

Gray, Donald. "The Incarnation: God's Giving and Man's Receiving." *Horizons* 1 (Fall 1974): 1-13.

John Paul II. "Holy Thursday 1983: Pope's Letter to Priests." *Origins* 12 (April 7, 1983): 687-690.

_____. "A Letter to Priests." *Origins* 8 (April 19, 1979): 687-690.

_____. "The Priest, the Man of Dialogue." *Origins* 12 (March 17, 1983): 640-642.

Kennedy, Eugene et al. "Stresses in Ministry." *Chicago Studies* 18 (Spring 1979): 5-132.

O'Collins, Gerald. "Theological Trends." *The Way* 16 (October 1976): 291-308.

O'Malley, John. "Reform, Historical Consciousness and Vatican II's Aggiornamento." *Theological Studies* 34 (1974): 573-601.